LET'S DO THAT AGAIN

Impromptu games to enjoy with your kids

Volume 1: Ready...Set...Go!

Tyler Bengtson

REDEVISED

For my children,
thank you for playing with me.

In honor of my parents,
who taught us how to love.

In memory of my brother Nick-Nack,
who had a heart for children and
a mind gifted with creating wonder.

Let's Do That Again: Impromptu games to enjoy with your kids
Volume 1: Ready...Set...Go!
1st edition   ISBN 9798366806350   (also available as an eBook)
Library of Congress Control Number: 2023909783
Copyright 2023
08705868950

Written and designed by Tyler Bengtson
Published by Redevised (*https://LDTA.redevised.com*)
To report errors, please send a note to *errata@redevised.com*

Goal buddy support from Jeff Cheek (and contribution of *Lost in Space*)
Canted Comic font by Nils Cordes

Apology to Ninjas, Shinobis, and Lunch Ladies
Some games herein refer to masters of martial arts and their art forms without much accuracy or cultural reverence. I've never met a ninja, but I imagine you are awesome. Sorry if I have offended you. Please don't hurt me. Similarly, the only lunch ladies I've ever known have been sweet, kind, and generous servants. Sorry I perpetuate a false stereotype in *No Fun for Anyone*, but hopefully we can all smile at its hyperbole.

S.G.D.

TABLE OF CONTENTS

FOREWORD

I love my kids, and I love to play with my kids. Over the years, we have created lots of games together, some heartwarming and hilarious, some quite forgettable. Through it all I've discovered a simple way to know when a game is "fun" for my kids; a genuine phrase emerged that became my litmus test to know if they enjoyed a new game. I would be playing with them on the family room floor, I would experiment with a wacky new game idea, and then I would listen carefully to their reaction. If they really liked it, if it was fun, they would instinctively say, "Let's do that again!" Such a simple phrase that answers such a complex question.*

At one point we were creating so many games that I started naming them and writing down brief summaries of the ones they enjoyed the most. After about six years of tracking our hijinks, I had over 300 of them, and I decided it was time to share these with other people: perhaps the tired parent with overly energetic kids, or the parent who is away from the kids most of the day and wants to make the time together count, or the dad who realizes he is not fun to play with (perhaps his dad did not play with him), or the grandparent who desires to demonstrate that people are more important than electronic devices, or the new dad who has no idea what joyful chaos lies ahead. My goal is to strengthen the father-child relationship by improving the quality of playtime together.

* Actually, the phrase changes with age. At 1.0 year of age, they would sign and say, "More." At about 1.5 years old, they would do that and say, "Ready, set, go" over and over. Sometime later, around 2 years old, "Let's do that again!" emerges naturally and stays for the rest of their childhood.

I am not an expert on games, or kids, or being a dad, but I am an expert on my kids. This book is a window into our lives: a curated list of our favorite games. And since all kids are different, I've included the practical techniques I've used so you can create your own games with your kids. While these games are original to us, I have no doubt many will seem familiar to you—that is part of the universal nature of play. But I will have failed in my purpose if, after reading this book, you are not left with at least a smile and a renewed desire for merrymaking with those you love. In truth, my prayer is that you will discover a new avenue of quality time with your kids and hear them (and yourself) say, "Let's do that again!"

Tyler Bengtson
August 28, 2019

This book is dedicated to my late brother, Nick. He was a magician (literally—he created and sold magic tricks that amazed not only people like us, but world-class magicians) who served young children as a preschool teacher at his church. He created impossible things, could glide effortlessly between the realms of seriousness and silliness, never letting age extinguish the enchantments of boyhood, nor knowledge rob him of being easily amazed. He was the best example I know of what a playful man should be.

INTRODUCTION

What I mean by "play" in this book

This is a book about playing games with children. While my kids and I have played sports, board games, video games, and the like, what I specifically mean by "play" in this book is impromptu, usually one-on-one games and amusements that are mutually amusing and do not require much more than time and the desire to delight.

So unlike organized sports teams, video games, or even a solitary kid jumping on a trampoline, this type of play is co-creative and simple, can be played almost anywhere, at any time, and without prerequisite tools or game pieces. It's free to play, and it's the type of thing you will remember fondly.

Organization of this book

Over the years, my kids and I have had so much fun creating games together. Not wanting to forget our games, I have kept a record of them all. Eventually, the curious nerd in me wanted to know why certain games were more fun than others, why some of our favorite games never seem to get old, and ultimately, how to create better games. So I closely analyzed all of our games* and wrote this book with the aim of providing a thoughtful, light-hearted resource for others like me.

* For example, by dissecting them down into smaller parts, identifying patterns, quantifying and comparing numerous factors, exploring the data through visualizations, and a countless amount of experimenting and testing with my kids.

My findings and conclusions are in part 2 of this book, which is a compendium of how to create your own games and how to be more fun to play with. Part 1 is a visual anthology of some of the best games we play. It does not attempt to catalog every possible game out there, but merely the ones we created and liked the most. All the games in part 1 include specific examples of the concepts described later in the book, such as the elements of fun, the stages of gameplay, improvisation starters, and more. So it is not cheating to look ahead in this book or to browse the glossary at the end.

Disclaimer 1: Be Gentle

Your children are precious, and their bodies are not for hurting, even if in the pursuit of fun. Be careful as you try out new games, and only ratchet your way up to crazier hijinks when you and your playmates are all ready. As a precaution, I have included a danger metric with each game, which provides a rough idea of how much potential destruction or distress it can cause.

Disclaimer 2: Be Tough

Playing with children is not for the frail-minded. Yes, in the pursuit of play you will at times need to crawl on your knees in your dress pants, and yes, at times your kids will climb on you when you are wearing your best shirt. Yes, they will:

- drool on your face, sometimes into your mouth, in a way you could not possibly have expected nor avoided
- yell into your ear like it's a megaphone
- crash into your shin—the bony part that only has 1 mm of skin protecting it
- realize it is funny to stick their fingers in your mouth and try to do that several times in a row
- end up throwing the ball over the wall into the neighbor's yard (the one whose name you still do not know)
- pull on your hair (what remains of it)
- jump off the edge of something for you to catch them, when you had no idea they were going to do that

And that is not even including the times you will:

- stub your toes on the leg of the sofa
- wonder if what you are about to do will irreparably damage your lumbar discs
- skin your knees
- step with full force on LEGOs, Cheerios, peas, and a number of other things that should never be stepped on
- throw the perfect pass, which they somehow miss, smashing into their face

Though if you do a great job, they will have a great time, but that means they will:

- Tantrum when gameplay is over
- Want to play with you every time you walk into the room
- Jump on your back anytime you bend over
- Jump on other people's backs when they bend over (sorry Grandma!)
- Expect even better games next time

If you really lean into the play, you will not be able to avoid most of this. You will need to decide if any of these inconveniences are more important than the special moment your kids might remember for the rest of their lives. I believe you will find that genuine, generous, creative play with your kids will yield some of the most worthwhile, character-defining, smile-inducing memories you will ever have.

PART 1

THE GAMES WE PLAY

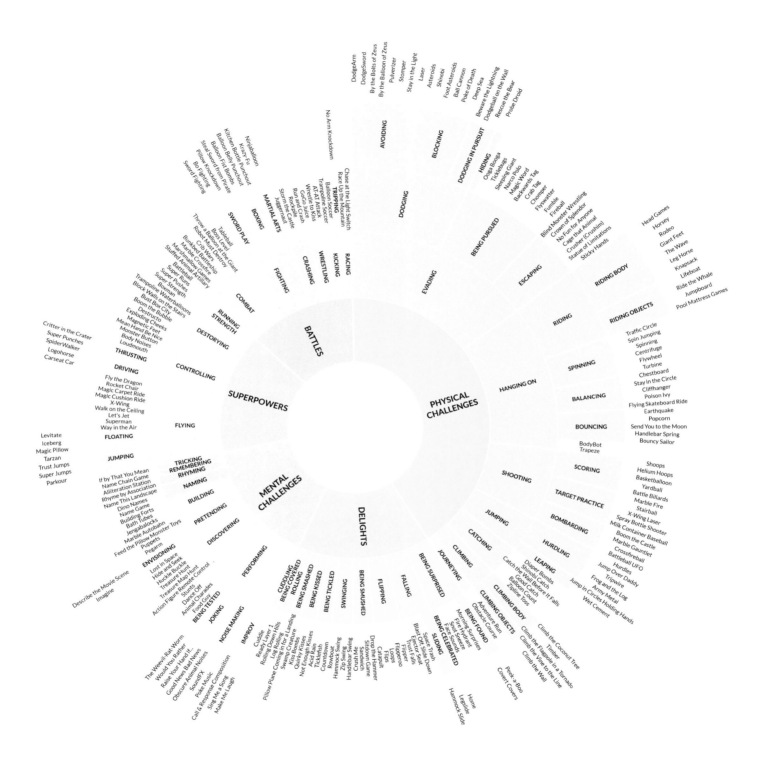

8

LEGEND

Categorization

After trying out several different ways of categorizing all the games we play, I found the best way was to focus on what I believe the primary delight for the child is. Those were then grouped into larger and more generic categories, ultimately resulting in five primary game types:

- **Physical Challenges**: Games where the focus is on using skill or strength to accomplish a goal
- **Mental Challenges**: Games where the most interesting challenge is more mental than physical
- **Battles**: Competitive games and contests with the goal of overcoming the opponent. These are generally head-to-head duels, without turn taking, where there is a struggle for victory, though generally not a prize.
- **Superpowers**: Activities where you augment the child's capabilities in a fantastic way, such as by removing limitations or amplifying current capabilities
- **Delights**: Simple amusements with the focus of giving the child temporary elation

Comparison Metrics

(each ranging from low to high)

- **Fun**: how much fun it is to play the game
- **Time**: the relative time commitment required to play the game
- **Complexity**: how difficult it is to set up, explain, and play the game
- **Danger**: how much of a safety risk there is in playing the game
- **Kid Effort**: how much exertion is required of the child
- **Exertion**: how much strength, focus, and effort is required of you

Ages

Minimum and maximum ages are suggested, based on these age groups:

- **Infant**: 2 months to 1 year, not yet walking
- **Toddler**: 1 to 3 years old
- **Preschooler**: 3 to 5 years old
- **School Age**: 6+ years old
- Otherwise, any age

Locations and Materials

Most of the games in this book are impromptu, but that does not mean you cannot use wantever materials happen to be within reach.

- **Carpet**: Activity is best played on a soft surface indoors, suitable for light tumbling
- **Couch**: This should be a well-padded couch or bed, as often the activity involves throwing your child onto it.
- **Trampoline**: All references to trampolines imply ones caged in by a net.
- **Doorway**: This generally implies a large threshold between rooms
- **Cushion**: A thick, dense couch cushion that you sit on, about 2 feet wide on each side. Pillows will generally not provide enough shock absorption for these activities.
- **Pillow**: A light, fluffy, bedtime pillow
- **Pillow Cushion**: A fluffy, usually square pillow that decorates a couch or chair
- **Crib**: A baby crib with barred walls on each side
- **Stuffed Animals**: Teddy bears, not taxidermy
- **Blocks**: Small toy building blocks. I prefer foam over wood for most games.
- **Balls**: This generally means the colorful, hollow, plastic balls you used to see in "ball pits" at fast food restaurants.
- **Air Mattress**: An inflatable queen-sized mattress, double-thick
- **Board Book**: A children's book with thick paperboard pages.

Players

Where the number of players are listed, that is the number of kids (in addition to you) playing the game.

Elements of Fun

These are described in Chapter 7, but to summarize briefly:

- **Anticipation**: Initiating the gameplay well for optimal fun
- **Enlivening**: Making it feel real with sound effects and theatrics
- **Tensity**: Balancing the right level of difficulty
- **Uncertainty**: Keeping things from being too predictable
- **Momentum**: Transitioning well within and between games

In these sections you will see a few acronyms, namely:

- **RSG**: Ready, Set, Go! (read more about this in Chapter 7)
- **SFX**: Sound effects

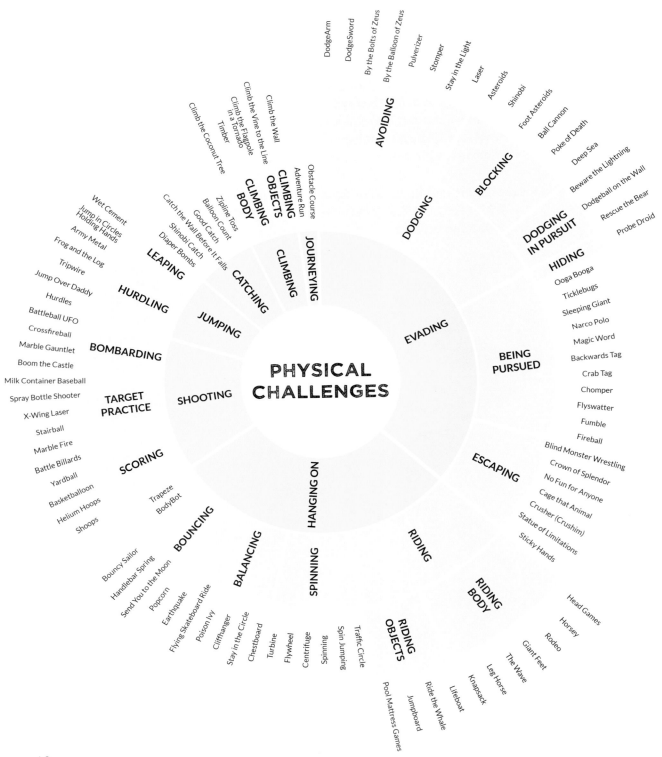

PHYSICAL CHALLENGES

JOURNEYING

CLIMBING
- CLIMBING BODY
  - Catch the Wall Before It Falls
  - Shinobi Catch
  - Diaper Bombs
- CLIMBING OBJECTS
  - Climb the Coconut Tree
  - Timber
  - Climb the Flagpole in a Tornado
  - Climb the Vine to the Line
  - Climb the Wall
  - Obstacle Course
  - Adventure Run
  - Zipline Toss
  - Balloon Count
  - Good Catch

CATCHING

AVOIDING
- DodgeArm
- DodgeSword
- By the Bolts of Zeus
- By the Balloon of Zeus
- Pulverizer
- Stomper
- Stay in the Light

DODGING
- Laser
- Asteroids
- Shinobi
- Foot Asteroids
- Ball Cannon
- Poke of Death
- Deep Sea

BLOCKING

DODGING IN PURSUIT
- Beware the Lightning
- Dodgeball on the Wall
- Rescue the Bear
- Probe Droid

HIDING
- Ooga Booga
- Ticklebugs
- Sleeping Giant
- Narco Polo
- Magic Word
- Backwards Tag
- Crab Tag
- Chomper
- Flyswatter
- Fumble
- Fireball
- Blind Monster Wrestling
- Crown of Splendor
- No Fun for Anyone
- Cage that Animal
- Crusher (Crushim)
- Statue of Limitations
- Sticky Hands

BEING PURSUED

EVADING

ESCAPING

RIDING
- RIDING BODY
  - Head Games
  - Horsey
  - Rodeo
  - Giant Feet
  - The Wave
  - Leg Horse
  - Knapsack
  - Lifeboat
  - Ride the Whale
- RIDING OBJECTS
  - Jumpboard
  - Pool Mattress Games

HANGING ON

SPINNING
- Traffic Circle
- Spin Jumping
- Spinning
- Centrifuge
- Flywheel
- Turbine
- Chestboard

BALANCING
- Stay in the Circle
- Cliffhanger
- Poison Ivy
- Flying Skateboard Ride
- Earthquake
- Popcorn

BOUNCING
- Send You to the Moon
- Handlebar Spring
- Bouncy Sailor
- Trapeze
- BodyBot

SCORING
- Shoops
- Helium Hoops
- Basketballoon
- Yardball
- Battle Billards
- Marble Fire
- Stairball

TARGET PRACTICE
- X-Wing Laser
- Spray Bottle Shooter
- Milk Container Baseball
- Boom the Castle

SHOOTING

BOMBARDING
- Marble Gauntlet
- Crossfireball
- Battleball UFO
- Hurdles
- Jump Over Daddy
- Tripwire
- Frog and the Log
- Army Metal
- Holding Hands
- Jump in Circles
- Wet Cement

HURDLING

LEAPING

JUMPING

CHAPTER 1
Physical Challenges

Games where the focus is on using skill or strength to accomplish a goal

ASTEROIDS

Defend yourself from incoming space debris

PHYSICAL CHALLENGES / EVADING / DODGING / BLOCKING

DEEP IN SPACE, THERE ARE . . .

ASTEROIDS!

MAKE A FIST AND SLOWLY HAVE IT FLY AT HER

SHE CAN EITHER AVOID IT

BOOM!

OR HIT IT WITH HANDS TO MAKE IT EXPLODE

IF IT HITS HER, THERE'S A BIG EXPLOSION WITH SHAKING AND TICKLING

 IF YOU'RE SITTING AND SHE RUNS, DON'T GO CATCH HER UNLESS YOU ARE TRANSITIONING TO A DIFFERENT GAME

! NO ROUGH TICKLING

! NO SMASHING HER FACE

ANTICIPATION:	"Deep in space, there are...asteroids!", full eye-contact, pause
ENLIVENING:	SFX, "Look out!", Announcing each change
TENSITY:	Speed, simultaneous asteroids, how easily deflected, near misses
UNCERTAINTY:	Order of elements, near misses
FLUIDITY:	End with destruction of mothership creating a black hole

FUN	
TIME	
COMPLEXITY	
DANGER	
KID EFFORT	
EXERTION	

MIN AGE:	Infant
MAX AGE:	School
LOCATION:	Any
MATERIALS:	-
PLAYERS:	1-3 kids

ELEMENTS

SPEED

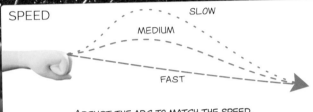

SLOW
MEDIUM
FAST

ADJUST THE ARC TO MATCH THE SPEED.
MAKE SURE TO INCLUDE ACCELERATION.

SIZE

TINY

- PINCH FINGERS
- SOFT WISP NOISE
- SLOW OR FAST

MEDIUM

- TIGHT FIST
- MISSILE SFX (BRRGHGH)
- BREAKS INTO TWO TINY ASTEROIDS

HUGE

- HANDS FORM BIG BALL
- LOW RUMBLE SOUND
- SLOW, BREAKS INTO TWO MEDIUM ASTEROIDS

TRAJECTORY

HEATSEEKER

CORKSCREW

HEATSEEKER: GOES UP AND AWAY, AND THEN RIGHT AT KID
CORKSCREW: SPIRALS IN TOWARD KID

RADIATION TYPES

X-RAY

GAMMA RAY

- FIRST FINGER POINTING AT KID
- VERY FAST, DIRECT POKE*

- FIRST FINGERS MAKE AN X,
- GOES THROUGH THINGS, SO CANNOT BE BLOCKED, MUST BE AVOIDED

Technically, gamma rays also go through your body like x-rays, but "gamma ray" sounds cooler than "alpha ray."

SPACECRAFT

ALIEN SPACESHIP

ALIEN MOTHERSHIP

- RAPIDLY WIGGLING FINGERS
- MOVES IN RANDOM PATH
- LANDS ON HEAD AND SUCKS OUT BRAINS

WHEN HIT, FALLS OUT OF SKY AND CRASHES TO THE GROUND

- LOUD LOW SOUND WHEN ENTERING
- HOVERS IN PLACE, DROPPING ALIENS
- CAN SHOOT MISSILES AND LASERS
- GOES DOWN A NOTCH WHEN HIT, BUT SLOWLY RISES BACK UP UNLESS THEY CONTINUE TO KNOCK IT TO THE GROUND, WHERE ITS EXPLOSION CAN SET OFF A BLACK HOLE

SPACETIME PHENOMENA

BLACK HOLE

WORMHOLE

"ITCHING" FINGER FLIES AT THEM, AIMING AT BELLY BUTTON

CAN TRANSPORT KID TO ANOTHER SPOT

- HOLD HANDS LIKE BALL AT STOMACH
- WIND SUCKING NOISE
- "NOTHING ESCAPES THE BLACK HOLE!"
- PULL KID TO YOU AND ROLL ON BACK
- THIS IS HOW THE GAME ENDS

ASTEROIDS

	Kid	Adult
Expectation	Fly through space	Barrage the kid
Challenge	Avoid getting hit	Sequencing more, various, faster elements
Fulfillment	Tickle-hug inside the black hole	Tickling a delighted kid

Small Play vs Big Play

- For pre-toddlers, you remain sitting throughout the gameplay.
  - The objective becomes purely about blocking.
  - Frequently narrowly miss her, minimizing her frustration at not being great at blocking yet.
  - My kids started knocking away asteroids at about 18 months old
- As the kid grows, she can evade the asteroids by rolling, jumping, or running out of the way.

Group Adaptation

- Taking turns, with kids sitting side by side facing you.
- Mix in some randomization, occasionally repeating, so they do not tune out when it is not their turn.

Variations

- Role reversal - Have kid chase you with asteroids

Deep Sea

- Anticipation: "Deep in the sea, there are..."
- Shark - Arms chomping
- Jellyfish - Hand with fingers pointing down, swooshing up motion
- Whale - Make huge, slow swallowing motion, sucking them in
  - Can be used to end the game, like black hole
  - Can burp them out to continue
- Fish - Flat hand undulating toward them
- Crab - Hand walks on ground, can pinch them
- Eel - Fingers make mouth at end of arm
- Electric Eel - Like eel, but they cannot touch it, only move away
- Sting Ray - Hands like a flat triangle, stinger comes out when close
- Snail - Slow crawler

Large-Scale Shooter Version

While playing asteroids, one of my kids decided he was in a spaceship and he did not have to hit the asteroids; he could just shoot them from this spaceship. This turned the game into one where I would run toward him from across the room and he would point and make shooting sounds to blast the asteroids.

Foot Asteroids

- If you have access to low-hanging bars, it is fun to play a variation where the kid hangs and kicks away asteroids.

Similar to **By the Bolts of Zeus** and **Pulverizer**

PROBE DROID

BEEP, BEEP, ZRRP..

SEARCHING FOR LIFEFORMS...

Description

· This is one we would play at bedtime in the dark.
· Close the door, turn off the lights, get out your smartphone, and turn on its built-in flashlight (or just use a regular flashlight).
· The smartphone is a probe droid that flies around the room looking for lifeforms while dictating a report of what it sees.
· The kids need to avoid being spotted by the probe droid.
· When they are caught in the light, go on high alert, fly in, and tickle them.

Variations

STAY IN THE LIGHT

· This is a game we would play while walking on a night hike.
· Shine a flashlight on the ground nearby and hold it there.
· They need to jump into and stay in the light, but soon after they get there, you move it to another spot.

Similar to **Lost in Space, Robot Must Destroy**

ANTICIPATION:	Turn spotlight on, say "PROBE DROID" in robot voice	
ENLIVENING:	Flying machine SFX. inspect random objects and give them technical names, say "life form" when you spot them	
TENSITY:	Flight speed, amount of them you need to see to capture	
UNCERTAINTY:	Erratic flight pattern, changing speed, direction	
FLUIDITY:	We generally transitioned to bedtime after this.	

FUN	
TIME	
COMPLEXITY	
DANGER	
KID EFFORT	
EXERTION	

MIN AGE:	Infant
MAX AGE:	School Age
LOCATION:	Any
MATERIALS:	-
PLAYERS:	1-2 kids

17

BEWARE THE LIGHTNING

Can they make it by without getting zapped?

PHYSICAL CHALLENGES / EVADING / DODGING / DODGING IN PURSUIT

ZZZZR ZZZR ZZZZZZR...

STAND IN DOORWAY MOVING ROBOTICALLY AND MAKING ELECTRICITY NOISES.

KID TRIES TO GET BY WITHOUT TOUCHING YOU. ONCE CLEAR, SHE LOOPS AROUND TO GO AGAIN.

BEWARE THE LIGHTNING!

OCCASIONALLY YELL OUT *"BEWARE THE LIGHTNING!"* AND CHASE HER.

BZZRG!

IF SHE TOUCHES YOU, SHE GETS ELECTROCUTED AND PUSHED BACK, UNABLE TO PASS.

ANTICIPATION: Getting in position
ENLIVENING: Sound effects (electricity zizzing, zapping, etc.)
INTENSITY: Speed, gap size, not facing them
UNCERTAINTY: Different patterns, occasional random movements
FLUIDITY: End by chasing, transition to chasing games

FUN	
TIME	
COMPLEXITY	
DANGER	
KID EFFORT	
EXERTION	

MIN AGE: Toddler
MAX AGE: School age
LOCATION: Doorway/hallway
MATERIALS: -
PLAYERS: 1-5 kids

LEVELS

LEVEL 1: STANDING STILL
MAKE THEM GO AROUND YOU

LEVEL 2: MOVING HANDS
MAKE THEM CRAWL UNDER YOU

LEVEL 3: LYING DOWN
MAKE THEM JUMP OVER YOU

LEVEL 4: CYCLING BACK & FORTH
MAKE THEM TIME IT RIGHT

Description

- For each turn, move in a repetitive, robotic pattern, and do not break out of the pattern to touch the kid.
- When the turn is over, switch it up to something slightly more challenging, occasionally doing a movement that is random and non-repetitive.
- Our favorite place to do this was in a wide entryway between rooms, and the kids could run around through the kitchen to get back in position. If you are in a hallway or doorway, you might need to let them back through or switch directions between iterations.

	Kid	Adult
Expectation	Get passed without making contact; otherwise, get electrocuted	Be an electric boundary wall
Challenge	Increasingly difficult levels	Sequencing more, various, faster maneuvers
Fulfillment	Outrun by lightning into a tickle-hug	Chasing and tickling a delighted kid

Group Adaptation

- Taking turns
- You can try to run two kids at once, if you dare.

Variations

- Backwards - turn around so you cannot see the kid coming. This helps keep you honest.
- Role reversal

NOT LOOKING
KEEPS YOU HONEST

COMBINATIONS

BLIND MONSTER WRESTLING

They wrestle you with your eyes closed

PHYSICAL CHALLENGES / EVADING / ESCAPING

READY...
[GRRR]...

SET...
[GRRRR]....

GO!

START ON YOUR HANDS AND KNEES. KEEP YOUR EYES CLOSED.

WITH YOUR EYES CLOSED, TRY TO GRAB HER

SHE TRIES TO JUMP ON YOUR BACK AND RIDE YOU, OR SHE JUST AVOIDS GETTING CAUGHT

IF YOU GET HER, TACKLE HER ON HER BACK AND KISS HER

ANTICIPATION:	Getting in position, RSG
ENLIVENING:	SFX [growls, snorts, long snarls, etc.], monster movements [wipe drool, quick jerky head movements]
TENSITY:	Speed, use feet, rolling, sweeping kicks they jump over
UNCERTAINTY:	Random movements [lunge, gallop, roll, up on knees, freeze listening], loud noises [yell, bear bark]
FLUIDITY:	Transition to lying down or chasing games

FUN	
TIME	
COMPLEXITY	
DANGER	
KID EFFORT	
EXERTION	

MIN AGE:	Toddler
MAX AGE:	-
LOCATION:	Carpet/Trampoline
MATERIALS:	-
PLAYERS:	1-3 kids

LEVELS

LEVEL 1: SLOW HAND REACHES THEY ALWAYS ESCAPE (BARELY)

LEVEL 2: THEY NEED TO JUMP ON YOUR BACK AND RIDE YOU

LEVEL 3: THEY NEED TO WRESTLE YOU DOWN

LEVEL 4: YOU CAN SEE (TEMPORARILY)

Description

- Originally we played this on a wide area rug (beware of coffee tables) and everyone had to stay on the rug. Later, we discovered a trampoline with a net is the ideal arena as it contains the play and reduces the pain-factor.
- Beware of fearless commando kids that go diving at you.

	Kid	Adult
Expectation	Ride the monster	Tackle the kid
Challenge	Savage blind monster is out to eat you	Crazy kid is trying to jump on your back
Fulfillment	Overcome by the monster into a tickle-hug	Laid flat by monkey-armed kid

Group Adaptation

I play this with up to three kids at the same time, which gets a bit dangerous with collisions. With four kids, they crash into each other and get hurt.

Variations

- Magic potion that lets you temporarily see
- Blind Monster Lunging - you wait in the center and can only attack by lunging out
- Role reversal

NO FUN FOR ANYONE

When fun is **NOT** allowed

PHYSICAL CHALLENGES / EVADING / ESCAPING

ANTICIPATION:	Start talking in old lunch lady voice	
ENLIVENING:	Voice, funny commentary [assign homework, everything is naughty, etc.], getting angrier	
TENSITY:	Ease of escape	
UNCERTAINTY:	What you'll say next (funny commentary), getting away	
FLUIDITY:	Transition to chasing games	

FUN	
TIME	
COMPLEXITY	
DANGER	
KID EFFORT	
EXERTION	

MIN AGE:	Toddler
MAX AGE:	School Age
LOCATION:	Any / Couch
MATERIALS:	-
PLAYERS:	1-3 kids

LEVELS

LEVEL 1: THEY MAKE REQUESTS AND GET DENIED

LEVEL 2: THEY TRY TO GET AWAY AND ARE BROUGHT BACK

LEVEL 3: THEY TRY TO TACKLE YOU AND SUCCEED

Description

- Falling into character is essential in this game. Probably half of the fun for the kids is hearing you talk in a funny voice and say ridiculously mean things.
- The first level is usually them asking for something basic and you rejecting them in the most extreme way possible. They will then try to do silly naughty things to make you angry, like run around and slap you on the bottom.
- Eventually they overcome you and (perhaps) soften your heart.

	Kid	Adult
Expectation	Upset the old lady	Keep the kid sitting perfectly still on couch
Challenge	Escaping her sneer and cold hands	Naughty kids have a mind of their own
Fulfillment	Being dragged back to the couch	Tackled by happy menaces

Group Adaptation

I play this with up to three kids at the same time, which might even be more fun that one-on-one play as their laughter is contagious.

Example Exchanges

- *No laughing! Stop giggling! No glee permitted! Sit still! No moving! Did you just blink at me?*
- *You are wayward and disorderly! Never in my 85 years have I seen such wanton display of mischievousness!*
- *10,000 pages of homework, due tomorrow!*

TICKLEBUGS

Your hands are alive... and out to get them

PHYSICAL CHALLENGES / EVADING / BEING PURSUED

WHAT'S THAT SOUND?

"TICK-A-TICK-A-TICK-A-TICK-LE"

YOUR HAND CRAWLS LIKE A SPIDER TO CATCH THE KID

HE CAN SMASH THE TICKLEBUG WITH HIS HANDS OR FEET

IF THE TICKLEBUG CATCHES HIM, HE GETS TICKLED

SPLAT!

"TICK-A-TICK-A-TICK-A-TICK-LE"

THEN THE NEXT TICKLEBUG COMES OUT FROM BEHIND

ANTICIPATION: "What's that sound?" Then make a skittering sound
ENLIVENING: SFX, movements that resemble intelligent creatures (they can avoid stomps, jump onto things, change speed, pause to think/plan)
TENSITY: Ease of smashing bug, speed
UNCERTAINTY: Bug movement, bug type, getting away
FLUIDITY: End with cuddle hug

FUN	
TIME	
COMPLEXITY	
DANGER	
KID EFFORT	
EXERTION	

MIN AGE: Infant
MAX AGE: School Age
LOCATION: Any
MATERIALS: -
PLAYERS: 1-2 kids

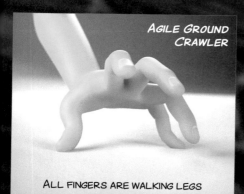

AGILE GROUND CRAWLER
ALL FINGERS ARE WALKING LEGS

THREE-TOED LAND SKIPPER
FAST FORWARD MOVER, SLOW SIDEWAYS

WINGED HARPOON HOPPER
HOPS ON MIDDLE FINGERS

LIGHT-FOOTED FIELD RUNNER
RUNS ON TWO FINGERS, RESTS ON BASE

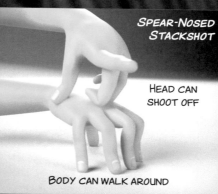

SPEAR-NOSED STACKSHOT
HEAD CAN SHOOT OFF
BODY CAN WALK AROUND

HORNED SNAIL SLIDER
SLIDES ON GROUND, HAS WRIGGLING EYES

SLITHERING STINGER

SLITHERS LIKE A SNAKE, TWITCHING STINGER

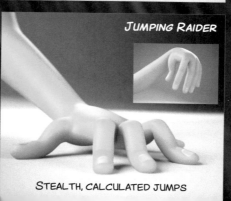

JUMPING RAIDER
STEALTH, CALCULATED JUMPS

FLUTTERFLY
WIDE, FLUTTERING WINGS; WOBBLY

TICKLEBUGS

Description

- Unless you are okay with them breaking your fingers, you need to anticipate their stomps and almost pre-flatten your hand.
- Do not endlessly avoid being stomped or they will get frustrated. Avoid them 0-3 times before allowing the inevitable.

	Kid	Adult
Expectation	Avoid getting tickled by smashing the ticklebugs	Tickle this kid
Challenge	Ticklebugs are quite agile	Creating realistic yet zany creatures
Fulfillment	Being tickled	Tickling a delighted kid

Age

- My youngest child was able to play at 7 months old
- At about 27 months old, my kids started making ticklebugs of their own.

Variations

Ticklefish ■ □ □ □ □ □ □

- Can be done in the bath with your hand or a toy
- See Deep Sea for ideas. Here are single hand adaptations:
  - Fish (slow, medium, fast) (flat vertical hand)
  - Eel (pointer)
  - Shark (biting hand)
  - Octopus/Jellyfish (wiggling fingers)
  - Starfish (fingers wide, settles down and latches on)
  - Crab (walking fingers)

Mean Hand, Be Nice ■ □ □ □ □ □ □

Toddler to preschool age
Superpowers / Controlling

- Start by being on the floor with your child, your elbow on the ground with your hand poised like a mean monster (i.e. with fingers like they are going around a ball).
- Wiggle fingers and rotate hand, making mean monster growl noises.
- When the child puts her hand into the monster's mouth, it eats and locks down on the her hand.
- She can then either:
  - Tickle the monster, which makes it laugh and open its mouth, or
  - Say "be nice," which makes the monster become gentle and friendly and cuddle her hand.
- Have the monster suddenly sneeze as a way of resetting into mean mode.

LEVELS

1 One hand at a time, easily squashed

2 Two hands, staggered or simultaneous

3 Two hands, incredible resistance to being crushed

BY THE BOLTS OF ZEUS

Zap your kids with lightning bolts from across the room

PHYSICAL CHALLENGES / EVADING / DODGING / AVOIDING

Description

- Standing in an open room with your child, pretend to throw a lightning bolt at her, forcing her to run away to avoid it.
- Once you pick a vector, you cannot change it, and it goes all the way until it hits something.
- You end up not aiming at her but where you think she will go next.
- If the lightning touches her, it turns into a tickle and you start over.

Similar to **Pulverizer**

Variations

By the Balloon of Zeus

- Similar idea, but use a balloon instead of your hand.

LASER

- Your hand is a calculating droid laser gun that hones in on where the kid is and shoots.
- While the kid is running away, you must chase the shot to whatever it hits (e.g. a wall).
- Reset and repeat, adjusting speed to match the kid's ability.

slow lightning

- With kid nearby, your fingers are lightning and slowly move toward her unless she runs.

ANTICIPATION:	RSG, talk like Zeus (e.g. "By the Bolts of Me!")	FUN	
ENLIVENING:	SFX (lightning sound, crashing sound), commentary	TIME	
TENSITY:	Speed of lightning, time between bolts	COMPLEXITY	
UNCERTAINTY:	Getting away or not	DANGER	
FLUIDITY:	Transitions well into other chasing games.	KID EFFORT	
		EXERTION	

MIN AGE: Toddler
MAX AGE: School Age
LOCATION: Any
MATERIALS: -
PLAYERS: 1-3 kids

FROG AND THE LOG
Jumping over the log that's rolling at you

PHYSICAL CHALLENGES / JUMPING / HURDLING

SHE IS A FROG,
AND YOU ARE A ROLLING LOG

TRY TO ROLL OVER HER
AS SHE TRIES TO JUMP OVER YOU

OCCASIONALLY TURN INTO A BOULDER
OR SNAKE AND ROLL/SLITHER AT HER

Description

It works best to have a defined "field" she has to run across, such as a rug or trampoline. She starts on one end, jumps over the log as it rolls across, then waits at the other end until the log comes rolling back across the field.

Group Adaptation

All the players must get across and wait together on the other side before the next iteration starts.

Age

- This can be too easy for older kids. Moving more randomly makes it more challenging for them; playing in a caged trampoline works well for that.
- For the little ones and for children with delayed motor processing, I generally slow down to a stop and let them crawl over me before continuing.

	Kid	Adult
Expectation	Jump over the log	Roll around at the kids
Challenge	Log sometimes moves unpredictably	Try to roll over them, choosing right speed and positioning to not crush kids
Fulfillment	Being tickled	Tickling a delighted kid

ANTICIPATION:	RSG	**FUN**	
ENLIVENING:	SFX (log crashing through the underbrush)	**TIME**	
TENSITY:	Speed of log (can slow/stop if needed)	**COMPLEXITY**	
UNCERTAINTY:	Randomizing direction and duration of rolling, becoming a boulder or snake	**DANGER**	
		KID EFFORT	
FLUIDITY:	End with cuddle hug, or transition to Log Rolling	**EXERTION**	

MIN AGE: Toddler
MAX AGE: Preschooler
LOCATION: Carpet, trampoline
MATERIALS: -
PLAYERS: 1-3 kids

CLIMB THE COCONUT TREE

Can she climb all the way to the top

UPPIE!

HOLD HANDS
FACING EACH OTHER

LIFT HER UP AS SHE
WALKS UP YOUR LEGS

AT THE TOP SHE CAN SIT OR STAND ON YOUR SHOULDERS.
THEN LET HER PLUNGE SO HER HEAD DANGLES BETWEEN YOUR LEGS.

Description

- I have found the best grip to be where her hands are grasping your thumbs while your hands are grasping her wrists.
- This one is quick and rapidly repeatable, though usually not more than a few times due to the effort involved.
- This is much harder to do with big kids. As they age out of this, consider substituting Timber.
- Similar to: **Timber**, **Flips**, and **Climb the Flagpole in a Tornado**

The Dismount

HOLDING HER WRISTS, DIP HER UPSIDE DOWN, THEN DROP HER FEET TO THE GROUND

ANTICIPATION:	"So you want to climb the coconut tree?"
ENLIVENING:	Encouraging commentary, sing a happy Jamaican song
TENSITY:	Amount of assistance provided, spin while she climbs
UNCERTAINTY:	Will she swoosh down or climb to the top?
FLUIDITY:	Naturally transitions to Head Games or Flips

FUN

TIME

COMPLEXITY

DANGER

KID EFFORT

EXERTION

MIN AGE: Toddler
MAX AGE: Preschooler
LOCATION: Any
MATERIALS: -
PLAYERS: 1 kid

Head Games

On your shoulders anything can happen

PHYSICAL CHALLENGES / HANGING ON / RIDING / BODY

Description
- When you are carrying your child on your shoulders, say "Ready... Set..." and wait for "go."
- Then do a sudden (but safe) motion, turning your walk into a roller coaster of a ride.
- Generally each iteration should be short, random, and a bit more exciting than the previous one.
- Don't have your child sit on your shoulders too long, it decreases blood circulation to her legs.

Age
- This game can start long before the child can walk.
- The upper age limit depends on the size of the child. For larger kids, avoid tilting.

Variations
Ratatouille: Kid grabs your hair (or ears) and pulls in the direction to go.

Tilt left	Tilt right	Lean forward	Lean backward	Run forward	Run backward

					Combinations
Dip down	Jump	Jiggle	Twist/spin left	Twist/spin right	• Spin jumps • Run while leaning • Run forward, then break, then reverse and break

ANTICIPATION:	RSG	**FUN**	**MIN AGE**: Infant
ENLIVENING:	Provide "Squier Crier" yells and exclamations	**TIME**	**MAX AGE**: School Age
TENSITY:	Duration of each iteration, combinations	**COMPLEXITY**	**LOCATION**: Any
UNCERTAINTY:	Random action each time	**DANGER**	**MATERIALS**: -
FLUIDITY:	Transition to songs or skipping	**KID EFFORT**	**PLAYERS**: 1 kid
		EXERTION	

30

ADVENTURE RUN

An urgent mission sought with dashing courage

- Traverse the Stepping Stones in Lava
- Seize the Sword!
- Fight the Guardian Toad
- Cross the Bridge
- Crawl through the cave
- Enter the castle and get the treasure

Description

- This game is a mixture of a treasure hunt and an obstacle course. After setting up the course, you get to call out what to do next.
- You can add interesting twists by changing up the order of items and repeating certain tasks where appropriate.
- Generally, you should have a treasure as the goal, and it needs to be clear that she must go through all the obstacles before obtaining it.

Group Adaptation

- Taking turns if there is more than one child
- Have those waiting help with resetting the course

Age

For older kids, this can be done for time, either having a time limit or working for a personal best time.

Example Flow

Using whatever items you have around, incorporate them into the theme. Here are some of the items we liked to use:

- Stepping stones over lava (pillows)
- Crawl through the cave (under dining chairs with blankets)
- Get the sword (toy sword)
- Run/swim
- Fight the minions (cushions)
- Kick down the door/wall (air mattress on edge)
- Jump across the bridge (air mattress, after it has been knocked down)
- Fight more minions (cushions)
- Enter the castle (made of cushions and blankets)
- Fight the guardian toad (a stuffed animal)
- Get the treasure
- Reset and start again

ANTICIPATION:	RSG	
ENLIVENING:	SFX, act as the "squire crier" ("Look out!", "Quick, grab the sword!", "Oh no! It's the Guardian Toad!")	
TENSITY:	Number of obstacles, difficulty of each obstacle	
UNCERTAINTY:	Changing up the order of obstacles, tampering with course	
FLUIDITY:	Call out what she must do next to keep her in flow	

FUN	
TIME	
COMPLEXITY	
DANGER	
KID EFFORT	
EXERTION	

MIN AGE:	Toddler
MAX AGE:	-
LOCATION:	Any
MATERIALS:	Various
PLAYERS:	1-3 kids

Narco Polo

Seize them before they laugh you to sleep

PHYSICAL CHALLENGES / EVADING / BEING PURSUED

IN A CONFINED SPACE...

CHASE HER TO TICKLE HER,

BUT HER LAUGHTER AND NOISE...

MAKE YOU INSTANTLY FALL ASLEEP.

ONCE IT IS QUIET AGAIN, GET BACK UP AND CONTINUE CHASING.

! DON'T ACTUALLY FALL ASLEEP (IF YOU CAN CONTROL IT)

ANTICIPATION:	RSG, gradual wake/stretch routine in each iteration
ENLIVENING:	SFX (snoring, hitting the ground), daunts and confusion remarks ("Huh? I must have fallen asleep. What was I doing? Oh yeah, I'm about to get you!"), slow-mo falling
TENSITY:	Play on knees, how loud they need to be to trigger sleep
UNCERTAINTY:	Almost falling asleep, adjusting sleep threshold
FLUIDITY:	They'll laugh when caught, which starts the next iteration.

FUN	
TIME	
COMPLEXITY	
DANGER	
KID EFFORT	
EXERTION	

MIN AGE:	Toddler
MAX AGE:	School Age
LOCATION:	Carpet
MATERIALS:	-
PLAYERS:	1-3 kids

Description

- This game works best when everyone must stay within a designated play area, such as an area rug.
- Especially with small kids, it makes sense to chase them while on your knees, as you will be falling down to sleep a lot.
- Wake up gradually, then go after them. Good enlivening here is important.
- When you capture and tickle them, they will laugh, which starts the next iteration.

	Kid	Adult
Expectation	Don't get caught	Chase the kids
Challenge	Not laughing	Catch them while they are silent
Fulfillment	Realizing the power of their laughter	Answering the age-old question: should I laugh, tickle, or sleep?

Group Adaptation

It is hard for two or more kids to both be quiet while playing, so you need to be flexible to balance pursuit and sleep intervals.

CAGE THAT ANIMAL

Don't let those silly animals get away

PHYSICAL CHALLENGES / EVADING / ESCAPING

YOU ARE A ZOOKEEPER, AND SHE IS AN ANIMAL IN THE ZOO...

...WHO ESCAPES!

YOU PURSUE

AND THROW HER BACK ON THE COUCH

CAGE THAT ANIMAL!

...ONLY TO SEE HER ESCAPE AGAIN.

ANTICIPATION:	Can start by picking up kid and saying "Cage that animal!"	
ENLIVENING:	Shock that animal escaped, yelling that you'll catch them	
TENSITY:	Ease of capture, head start time you give them	
UNCERTAINTY:	Getting away, random animal characters	
FLUIDITY:	After returning them, saying enticing comments like: "I'm glad that will never happen again"	

FUN	▓▓▓▓▓▓
TIME	▓▓▓
COMPLEXITY	▓▓▓▓
DANGER	▓▓▓▓
KID EFFORT	▓▓▓▓▓
EXERTION	▓▓▓▓▓

MIN AGE:	Toddler
MAX AGE:	School Age
LOCATION:	Couch
MATERIALS:	-
PLAYERS:	1-3 kids

Description

I pretend I am a zookeeper on patrol, and when I return an animal, I turn around and start to walk away.

	Kid	Adult
Expectation	Be an animal and escape the zoo	Keep the animals in the zoo
Challenge	The zookeeper chases you	Catching runaway animals
Fulfillment	Getting thrown back into the zoo	Funny animal enactments

Group Adaptation

With more than one kid, it is more interesting to take turns and to have each kid call out which animal he is pretending to be before escaping.

Age

Younger kids do not even need to pretend to be an animal; it is fun just to escape and be chased.

Chestboard

Surfing on your chest

PHYSICAL CHALLENGES / HANGING ON / BALANCING

HE STANDS ON YOUR CHEST
HOLDING YOUR HANDS

THEN HE SURFS WITH MINIMAL SUPPORT.

WITHOUT TOUCHING HIM, FLING YOUR HANDS
TO DAUNT HIM INTO FALLING.

Description

- Make sure they do not stand on your stomach—they should stand on your rib cage. Also beware of them jumping straight down on top of you.
- Sometimes I lift my knees up behind them to give them a surface to steady themselves with or to sit upon.

Levels

1. Holding hands (two, and then one)
2. No hands
3. Battery of (near) assaults to make him fall

Age

- Can start well before they can walk (my son did well with help at 4 months old), but they tend to have more fun starting around 12 months old.
- They will not be able to stand without help until after 24 months old.

Example Assults

- Blow on feet (ocean breeze)
- Tickle toes and legs (fish bites)
- Almost poke
- Slicer arms that almost make contact
- Move chest up and down (ocean waves)
- Slightly rotate of chest (ocean waves)

Variations

Have him play other games on your chest, using balance as a way to increase the tensity of that game (e.g. catch).

Similar to **Levitate**

ANTICIPATION:	RSG
ENLIVENING:	SFX, ocean movements, assaults
TENSITY:	Hand supports, assaults
UNCERTAINTY:	Timing and speed of assaults
FLUIDITY:	Transition to cuddling or Flipper

FUN
TIME
COMPLEXITY
DANGER
KID EFFORT
EXERTION

MIN AGE:	Infant
MAX AGE:	Preschooler
LOCATION:	Any
MATERIALS:	-
PLAYERS:	1 kid

TIMBER

Climb me to the top

YOU ARE A TREE, AND SHE CLIMBS YOUR BRANCHES.

AFTER SHE LEAVES A BRANCH, CREATE A NEW ONE HIGHER UP.

CRRRRACK

NEAR THE TOP, MAKE WOOD CRACKING NOISES...

...AND EVENTUALLY FALL OVER ONTO THE COUCH TOGETHER SAYING "TIMBER!"

TIMBER!

Description

- Branches can break too if she makes a poor footing choice.
- You can add time pressure (branch breaks if too slow).
- Often I would let them climb to the top and touch the ceiling.

ANTICIPATION:	Getting in position as a tree by couch
ENLIVENING:	SFX (tree growing branches, cracking branches, falling tree), lumberjack dwarf chopping down tree
TENSITY:	Positioning the holds, degree of help provided for footings
UNCERTAINTY:	When tree will fall, where next hold will be
FLUIDITY:	Make sure the next hold is ready as soon as they step off of one

FUN
TIME
COMPLEXITY
DANGER
KID EFFORT
EXERTION

MIN AGE:	Toddler
MAX AGE:	School Age
LOCATION:	Couch
MATERIALS:	-
PLAYERS:	1 kid

Crown of Splendor

No thief gets away with stealing the king's crown

PHYSICAL CHALLENGES / EVADING / ESCAPING

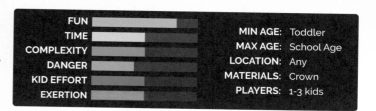

ANTICIPATION: Fanfare anthem, "I am the king, this is my kingdom, and I sit on my throne."

ENLIVENING: King's exclamations

TENSITY: Ease of allowing them to steal the crown, speed of chase

UNCERTAINTY: Getting away

FLUIDITY: Transitions well into chasing games

FUN	
TIME	
COMPLEXITY	
DANGER	
KID EFFORT	
EXERTION	

MIN AGE: Toddler
MAX AGE: School Age
LOCATION: Any
MATERIALS: Crown
PLAYERS: 1-3 kids

FANFARE

♩ = 80

Maestoso

Piano*

ff

* Pretending to be trumpets and French horns

Description

- Set up by getting a toy crown or helmet. Optionally build a dungeon from couch cushions and pillows.
- I always go over to the piano and play this game's fanfare anthem, which beckons the kids in.
- After saying my opening declaration, I sit down. The kids then sneak up slyly and try to steal the crown.
- You can make it easy or difficult to steal, but when they do steal it, you make a big deal as they run away.
- When you catch the kids, you can either pardon them and reset, or you can put them in the dungeon, from which they will then escape to steal your crown again.
- It is important to stay in character as the King, constantly making pompous, aristocratic statements.

	Kid	Adult
Expectation	Steal the crown	Let the kid steal the crown
Challenge	Being chased	Catching the thief
Fulfillment	Getting caught	Playing the king

Example "Over-Kingly" Exclamations

- "I am the king, this is my kingdom, and I sit on my throne" – starts each iteration
- "Ah, young peasant child yonder, do you wish to have audience with your king?"
- "It is right and proper that you admire my nobility."
- "Have no fear youngling—yes, you are in the presence of greatness, but I rule with a firm yet gentle hand."
- "She stoooooole the crown!" – each time kid steals crown
- "Mark my words, justice always prevails in the end."

Group Adaptations

- If one kid is dominating the play by always stealing the crown, the king can deflect his attempts so that others have a chance to steal.
- It helps to have a "dungeon" to put captured kids into while you chase the others.

Variations

- Reverse roles, so the kid gets to be the king
- King sleeps and crown is stolen while sleeping

Sleeping Giant

If you wake a kissing giant, he just might catch you and kiss you

PHYSICAL CHALLENGES / EVADING / BEING PURSUED

LIE ON THE FLOOR, PRETENDING TO SLEEP

KIDS CLIMB ON, TRYING TO WAKE YOU

PRETEND TO BRUSH THEM OFF IN YOUR SLEEP

EVENTUALLY YOU WAKE UP AND YAWN...

...AND SEE THE KIDS

...MAKE LOUD KISSING NOISES

...AND CHASE THEM, MAKING STRONGER KISSING NOISES AS YOU GET CLOSER.

WHEN YOU CATCH ONE, TICKLE-KISS HER AND SAY "I LOVE YOU!"

THEN 'SEE' THE OTHER KID AND START TO CHASE HIM.

ANTICIPATION:	Getting in position and snoring	
ENLIVENING:	Accelerating crescendo of kissing sounds, waking up actions	
TENSITY:	Ease of being woken, speed of chase	
UNCERTAINTY:	How do I to wake the giant? Is the giant awake?	
FLUIDITY:	Transitions well to tumbling games like Flipper and Chestboard.	

FUN	
TIME	
COMPLEXITY	
DANGER	
KID EFFORT	
EXERTION	

MIN AGE:	Infant
MAX AGE:	Preschooler
LOCATION:	Any
MATERIALS:	-
PLAYERS:	1-2 kids

Description

- In the first stage of the game, the kids try to wake you from a deep sleep. Make this challenging for them by brushing them off, almost waking, and rolling over.
- We also called this Kissing Giant.

	Kid	Adult
Expectation	Wake the giant	Pretend to sleep and get accosted
Challenge	Escape from the giant	Chasing the kid
Fulfillment	Getting caught and kissed	Joy of kissing a laughing kid

Group Adaptations

- Since you can only really chase one child at a time, other kids tend to hover by and anticipate their turn. Once you have kissed the escaping kid, lock in on the next and continue the chase.
- If there is only one kid, you can fall asleep kissing or transition to another game.

Age

Infants seem to instinctively understand this game from early on.

Variations

Magic Word *Toddler to school age*

- Lie still on the ground or sit like a statue, and think of a word
- Kid needs to guess the word
- Chase kid as soon as he says the magic word
- Reset and pick new word
- Variation: Stand, and have each incorrect word slowly bring you closer to the ground

Similar to:

- Ooga Booga
- Monster Button

OOGA BOOGA

What did you say? Chase you like a caveman?

PHYSICAL CHALLENGES / EVADING / BEING PURSUED

OOGA BOOGA?

WHAT DID YOU SAY?

OOGA BOOGA

OOOO-GAAAA BOOOO-GAAAA!

OOGA! OOGA! OOGA BOOGA!

CATCH HER, HUG HER, KISS HER, AND TELL HER YOU LOVE HER.

ENLIVENING:	Chanting "ooga" as you run, swiping at her hair and back
TENSITY:	Ease of escape
UNCERTAINTY:	Getting away
FLUIDITY:	After the kiss, restart with "What did you say?" as soon as she says "Ooga booga." You can also transition to Space Trash.

FUN		
TIME		
COMPLEXITY		
DANGER		
KID EFFORT		
EXERTION		

MIN AGE:	Toddler
MAX AGE:	School Age
LOCATION:	Any
MATERIALS:	-
PLAYERS:	1-3 kids

Description

- Simple as it is, this is one of our all-time favorites. It is also one that my older kids started to spontaneously play with my younger ones—a heartwarming moment for me.
- Like other chasing games, you want to be close behind, giving the sense that each move and decision they make matters. I would chase them noisily, with loud footsteps and constantly call out "Ooga," and occasionally I would swipe at their backs, as if I almost grabbed them.
- Follow them wherever they go. We looped through a natural circular path of our kitchen, dining room, then family room, but even still, I would follow them under dining table chairs, under tables, and around furniture.
- The time to capture them is when you are approaching a soft landing zone (e.g. near a couch or carpeted area) and before they get tired of running.

Group Adaptations

- Chase one kid at a time, the one who you ask "What did you say?"
- After you catch and kiss one kid, another will yell "Ooga booga", and you immediately focus all your attention on him—"What did you say?"

Similar to

- Sleeping Giant

43

ANTICIPATION: RSG

ENLIVENING: SFX (hit sounds), play Shinobi music in background

TENSITY: Block speed, time between firing, throwing multiple at once, distance, attack method (e.g. punch, slice, kick)

UNCERTAINTY: Randomize target and speed

FLUIDITY: Play until you run out of blocks, then transition to Shoops

		MIN AGE:	Toddler
FUN		MAX AGE:	-
TIME		LOCATION:	Carpet
COMPLEXITY		MATERIALS:	Blocks
DANGER		PLAYERS:	1-3 kids
KID EFFORT			
EXERTION			

Description

- We use foam building blocks (various sizes, shapes, and colors) because they are soft on the hands and furniture and they are easier to clean up since they do not roll far. Play balls or small stuffed animals can also work.
- You can play for time, number of throws, or until you run out of blocks.
- Optimal throw timing is highly dependent on the skill and reflexes of the child, but the sweet spot is to already have it in the air while she is just finishing with the previous block.

	Kid	Adult
Expectation	Defend yourself	Throw lots of blocks
Challenge	More and more blocks come flying	Calibrating timing, targets, and speed
Fulfillment	Attacking stuff and being allowed to make a mess	Getting into a Zen-like flow

Levels

- Sitting on couch, single fire
- Standing – hit and kick
- Rapid fire
- Multi-fire (throw multiple at a time, throw using both hands)

Example Moves

- Sway
- Duck
- Swat
- Punch
- Slice
- Elbow
- Kick
- Knee

Group Adaptations

You can do this by rapidly throwing at multiple kids. Randomize it to keep it interesting.

Variations

- Change roles

SHINOBI CATCH ■ ■ ■ ■ ■ ■

Toddler or older
Physical Challenges / Catching

- Facing each other across the room, take turns throwing foam blocks with full force at each other.
- Each player much try to catch the block with minimal movement, ideally by only subtly moving one hand, and without flinching or even taking your eyes off the other person.
- Similar to **Diaper Bombs**

45

LIFEBOAT

Sail the seas, but don't fall out of the boat

PHYSICAL CHALLENGES / HANGING ON / RIDING / OBJECTS

ALL ABOARD!

THE COUCH CUSHION ON YOUR LEGS IS A BOAT.

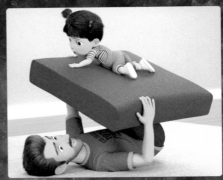

SHE NEEDS TO STAY ON THROUGH STORMY WAVES, HURRY BACK ON IF SHE FALLS OVERBOARD,

SHARK!

AND FEND OFF SEA CREATURES.

ANTICIPATION:	"All aboard!"			
ENLIVENING:	SFX (waves, wind, sea creature noises, crashing), movements (rocking, tilting, etc.)			
TENSITY:	Degree of movement, creatures that bite and pull			
UNCERTAINTY:	Randomize order of events			
FLUIDITY:	Falling leads right back to restarting			

FUN		MIN AGE: Toddler
TIME		MAX AGE: School Age
COMPLEXITY		LOCATION: Carpet
DANGER		MATERIALS: Cushion
KID EFFORT		PLAYERS: 1 kid
EXERTION		

Description

- When the child falls, build tension by bringing out sea creatures to chase and eat her.
- If you feel so inclined, sing her a sea chantey.

Levels

1. Gentle waves – Subtle rocking for introduction, but it can build up to a rough storm
2. Sea creatures approach
3. Storm with rough waves – rock and tilt dramatically

Example Sea Creatures

Shark
Flat hand as fin, until it pounces out of water as a chomping hand

Crab
Crawls onboard and pinches

Eel
Chomping hand wriggling about. Can also be a sea snake.

Mean Sea Lion
Make loud grunting noises and try to bump kid off boat, then lie down and sleep on it.

The Kraken
Both arms come out of water. No one escapes the Kraken.

Variations

Ride the Whale ■ ■ ■ ■ ■ □

- Instead of a cushion, use an air mattress
- Can be played with multiple kids at once

Magic Cushion Ride ■ ■ ■ ■ □ □

- Start in same position, with the child lying on a cushion on your shins.
- The child has arms out while you rock your legs about and sing "A Whole New World."
- For younger children, I do a simpler "Magic Carpet Ride" without a cushion (right on my legs). My youngest enjoyed this around 4 months old.

jumpboard ■ □ □ □ □ □

- Lie on your back with knees folded up and with a big pillow on your shins.
- Have a few floor pillows to the side, and one under your hips as the kids get older.
- The child runs and jumps onto your shins.
- You wiggle her back and forth and then dump her on the floor pillows.

The Wave

- The impromptu version of Jumpboard, where you do not have any cushions and the kids jump onto your shins.
- You rock the child forward and back in bigger and bigger waves until you both fall over.

Similar to: Storm the Castle, Row the Boat

DodgeArm

Can they avoid getting hit?

PHYSICAL CHALLENGES / EVADING / DODGING / AVOIDING

48

				MIN AGE:	Toddler
ANTICIPATION:	Smack talk, crack knuckles		**TIME** ▬▬	**MAX AGE:**	-
ENLIVENING:	SFX (inordinate amount of martial art grunts and ha's)		**COMPLEXITY** ▬	**LOCATION:**	Any
TENSITY:	Speed of attack, how close you aim		**DANGER** ▬	**MATERIALS:**	-
UNCERTAINTY:	Which attack is next? Mix up speeds and timings. Break anticipation by changing things up mid-attack.		**KID EFFORT** ▬▬▬	**PLAYERS:**	1-3 kids
FLUIDITY:	If your attack lands, work it into a tickle and start over.		**EXERTION** ▬▬		

Description

- Unlike battle games, the kid is not trying to attack back. The satisfaction comes from avoiding the attacks.
- You will want to train your kid on how to anticipate which direction to go based on how your attack starts. You can of course surprise them with changing course mid-attack.
- This game only seems to get better with age.

Example Moves

 Slash down-left — Duck away

 Slash down-right — Duck away

 Slash straight down — Move aside

Slash high horizontal — Duck down

 Jump — Slash low horizontal

Slash down with both hands — Slide between

 Point straight into — Sway

Group Adaptation

Like most games, I prefer this one-on-one, but this can be adapted for multiple kids if you are able to keep them close together and divvy up your attacks between them. I have played with up to six on a trampoline.

Variations

DODGESWORD

- Use a pool noodle as a sword (thicker is better for slower speed and thus easier reaction time).
- For younger kids you can use a pillow instead, as it is much slower and makes a satisfying smack sound.
- Use a hose or rope to mark a circular boundary, because it is less fun when people just run away.
- The kid can have a shield (e.g. ball) to protect herself.
- You can make the kid's objective to touch the head of the person holding the sword without getting hit.
- You can switch sides (e.g. if you knock the ball-shield loose, run after it and if you get it, switch sides).
- If the sword hits the opponent, you lose that limb, and the game is over when you have no limbs left.

DodgeSnake ▬ ▬ ▬ ▬ ▬

- Similar to DodgeSword, but the pool noodle slithers near the ground and the kid needs to jump over it.
- Occasionally the snake tries to strike up in the air.

DodgeFist ▬ ▬ ▬ ▬ ▬   Similar to DodgeArm, but use your fists with boxing technique.

DodgeWater ▬ ▬ ▬ ▬ ▬

- Go outside and put an attachment on the water hose that allows you to shoot a long beam.
- Have the kid stand far away. Act like you have a long sword. The kid must dodge it or otherwise get wet.
- You can also make them "dance"... just because.

CLIFFHANGER

Climb the wall but don't fall

PLAN   RUN!   JUMP!   CLIMB!   AND ONCE SHE IS LYING ON TOP, WIGGLE IT TO MAKE HER FALL.

ANTICIPATION: RSG

ENLIVENING: Vicarious SFX (grunts, hitting wall, falling yells), squire crier

TENSITY: Mattress climbing angle, amount of wiggling, interference while climbing (e.g. wiggle)

UNCERTAINTY: When and how much interference

FLUIDITY: Inevitably, you wiggle hard enough that the kid falls, allowing the game to reset or convert to a variation

FUN	▓▓▓▓▓
TIME	▓▓
COMPLEXITY	▓▓
DANGER	▓▓▓▓
KID EFFORT	▓▓▓
EXERTION	▓▓

MIN AGE: Toddler
MAX AGE: School Age
LOCATION: Carpet
MATERIALS: Air Mattress
PLAYERS: 1-3 kids

Description

- This is actually a combination of two games we would play (Climb the Wall and Cliffhanger), but they usually were combined unless there were larger groups.
- The mattress needs to be large and extra thick; otherwise, there is not enough of a ledge for the kid to lie down on. We used a queen-sized, double thick mattress that already had a hole in it.
- It is also good to have the mattress slightly deflated, as this allows it to bend a bit while the kid climbs.
- You should put a scattering of couch cushions and pillows at the base of the wall so the kid has something soft to land on.

	Kid	Adult
Expectation	Climb the wall and hang on	Kid will climb the wall
Challenge	The wall wiggles	Wiggle her off without hurting her
Fulfillment	Getting to the top, falling on cushions	Making her fall (safely)

Group Adaptation

Only one kid should go at a time. The others can wait in a line and take turns.

Age

For younger kids who found climbing too difficult, I would angle the wall like a ramp so they could get to the top. When they reached the top, I would straighten it back up.

Variations

Catch the Wall Before It Falls ▓ ▓ ▓ ▓ ▓ ▓ *At least preschool age*

- Similar setup, but the mattress is up against a wall.
- After RSG, you let the figurative wall (i.e. the mattress) start to fall.
- The kid runs from across the room as the wall slowly falls.
- The kid tries to catch the wall and put it back upright before it hits the floor.
- You can optionally combine this with Climb the Wall and Cliffhanger.

BOOM THE CASTLE

Can you build it faster than they destroy it?

PHYSICAL CHALLENGES / SHOOTING / BOMBARDING

You have foam or wood blocks for building.

You build a castle as fast as you can.

She has lots of play balls for throwing.

She stands at a distance and tries to knock it down.

As they knock things down, you rebuild.

ANTICIPATION: RSG

ENLIVENING: SFX (crash of bombs, crash of towers falling), commentary

TENSITY: Distance, speed of rebuild, number of layers (thickness of walls, barricades)

UNCERTAINTY: Will this throw knock it down?

FLUIDITY: If a total knockdown, you can concede or continue.

FUN	▮▮▮▮▮	
TIME	▮▮▮	**MIN AGE:** Toddler
COMPLEXITY	▮▮	**MAX AGE:** -
DANGER	▮▮	**LOCATION:** Carpet
KID EFFORT	▮▮▮	**MATERIALS:** Blocks, balls
EXERTION	▮▮	**PLAYERS:** 1-3 kid

Description

- If you do not have play balls, you can use stuffed animals or foam blocks.
- We sometimes played with there also being one big ball that rolls ("Cannonball!"), and I would set up ramps to try to stop it.
- Inevitably you will get hit in the head with items. The more you say "Ouch", the more they will aim for you.
- The kids eventually run out of balls, and they need to go collect them. I usually would roll the ones in the build site back to them to help.

	Kid	Adult
Expectation	Knock down the castle	Build up the castle
Challenge	The castle is constantly being rebuilt	Incoming cannonballs!
Fulfillment	Bombarding things	Rapidly building ephemeral structures

Levels

- Knock down the castle as you build
- Have a "King" (e.g. army man) that is the target (the game is over when he is knocked down)
- Place a barricade in their way (e.g. cushions)

Group Adaptation

Works great as a group game, with the kids cooperating on the attack.

Variations

- Role Reversal: You can switch sides and let the kids build.

Example Commentary

- "Heave Ho!"
- "Cannonball!"
- "You boomed my castle!"
- There can be lots of smack talk about misses.

Age

- For infants, see Destructo and Boom the Bubble.
- Older kids will need to be farther away (and not throw hard objects).

DESTRUCTO ▮▮□□□□

Age: *Infant to toddler*
Materials: *Blocks on carpeted area*

- In this game, you are building structures with blocks and the baby is crawling in and destroying them.
- You need to build them faster than he destroys them.
- For my kids, 9 months old was a great age for this game.

BOOM THE BUBBLE ▮□□□□□

Age: *Infant to school age*
Materials: *Bubbles*

- In this game, you are blowing medium to large sized bubbles, while the kid, pretending to know martial arts, is punching them with his fists or hitting them with a bat.
- Adjust the difficulty by making more bubbles or smaller bubbles.

Similar to **Battleball**

53

MARBLE FIRE

Send the marble into the target

PHYSICAL CHALLENGES / SHOOTING / TARGET PRACTICE

Description

- You will want several marbles for this game, as restocking detracts from the fun.
- We played this on a hardwood floor, but other smooth surfaces could probably work, such as a long dining table.
- Borders should enclose the entire playing field (loose marbles will roll around) and be strong enough to not be blasted away by errant marbles. In a pinch, use a blanket.
- We usually played with a small goal (only slightly bigger than the marble) so that it was exciting when someone scored. For bigger goals, the goals should be farther away.

Levels

- Take turns shooting
- Rapid fire shooting, be the first to score
- Kid shoots and you send a marble after it to knock it away

Variations

MARBLE AUTOBAHN ■ ■ ■ □ □ ■ ■

- Set up a course for the marble to roll along (edges, curves, jumps, etc.)
- Roll a marble along the course and try to get it into the target at the end.

Marble Gauntlet ■ □ ■ □ ■ □

- Set up a tower and several mini-towers around it (e.g. wood blocks or LEGOs).
- Make sure to have a back wall to stop the marbles.
- Vigorously roll marbles, trying to knock down the tower.
- You can take turns or go "rapid fire" style.

MARBLE CROSSFIRE ■ ■ ■ □ ■ ■

- Be at opposite sides of the playing field.
- Try to score in the other's goal by launching lots of marbles (one at a time).

Similar to **Stairball** and **Boom the Castle**.

		MIN AGE:	Toddler
ANTICIPATION: RSG	**FUN**	**MAX AGE**:	-
ENLIVENING: SFX (crash sounds), commentary	**TIME**	**LOCATION**:	Floor
TENSITY: Having obstacles, distance to target	**COMPLEXITY**	**MATERIALS**:	Marbles
UNCERTAINTY: Will I make it?	**DANGER**	**PLAYERS**:	1 kid
FLUIDITY: Reload after you have fired all your marbles, then rearrange the playing field for the next iteration.	**KID EFFORT**		
	EXERTION		

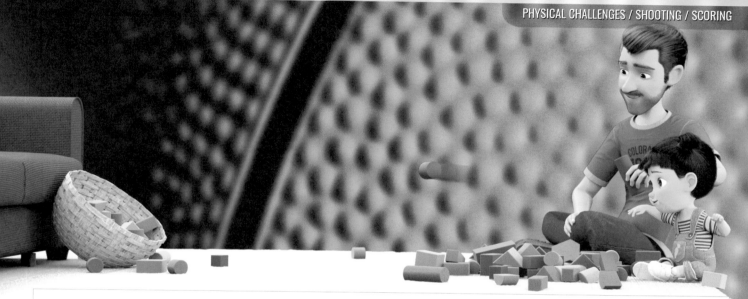

Shooting hoops with whatever you've got

SHOOPS

Description

- We often use foam blocks because they do not roll and they are already in a basket at our house.
- I tilt the basket forward so we can shoot directly at the basket. Young kids tend to throw at the basket rather than lofting into it.
- It works well to have two baskets: one to pull balls out of and one to shoot into. When the former is empty, switch baskets.
- I use a simplified version of this game as a way of getting the kids to clean up a room littered with toys or stuffed animals.

Levels

- Just try to make it
- Make bounce shots and other trick shots
- Make X number in a row into the basket
- Make X number in 60 seconds

Similar to

- Shinobi

Variations

Whiteboard Shoops ▪ ◻ ▪ ◻ ▪ ◻ ▪
At least preschool age
Using a wall and balls

- Draw baskets on a whiteboard (or tape papers to wall) with different points on each one.
- Take turns "shooting" at the baskets, seeing who can get the most points.

Football Shoops ▪ ▪ ◻ ◻ ◻ ◻ ◻
School age
Using a bucket and football

- Set a large bucket or dumpster in the grass.
- Take turns throwing a football into the bucket.

YARDBALL ▪ ◻ ◻ ◻ ◻ ◻ ◻
Preschool to school age
Using crawling tubes and balls

- Set a large crawling tube or bucket in the center of a grassy yard.
- Shoot balls into the tube, either taking turns or having teams.

ANTICIPATION:	RSG	
ENLIVENING:	SFX	
TENSITY:	Distance from basket	
UNCERTAINTY:	Will the shot go in?	
FLUIDITY:	Play till out of blocks, then shoot in the ones you missed, then switch out the full basket with the empty one.	

FUN	
TIME	
COMPLEXITY	
DANGER	
KID EFFORT	
EXERTION	

MIN AGE:	Toddler
MAX AGE:	-
LOCATION:	Any
MATERIALS:	Balls/blocks
PLAYERS:	1-3 kids

TRAFFIC CIRCLE

Round and round we go, until we randomly stop

PHYSICAL CHALLENGES / HANGING ON / SPINNING

Description

- Start by facing each other on opposite sides of a room.
- Have kid choose one of your hands by pointing at it.
- Say "Green light!", run together, and clasp opposite hands.
- While spinning, randomly yell out a color of a traffic light.

Example Colors

- Green - Go!
- Yellow - Slow
- Red - Stop!
- Blue/Purple - Backwards
- Black - Backwards FAST

Group Adaptation

- You can add a second kid into the mix by having him hold your other hand.
- You can make a chain with additional kids, but that falls apart rapidly.

Variations

Spinning ▮▯▯▯▯▯▯ *Toddler to school age*

- This is the basic version (which we play the most).
- After you run and clasp hands, you spin and spin, occasionally switching hands and directions. Spin until the kid cannot hang on and falls to the ground.
- For enlivening, accelerate, crescendo, and yell "We're spinning!"

SPIN JUMPING ▮▯▯▯▯▯▯

- Integrate in timed jumps as you go around (e.g. to a song or counting).
- Or set down objects that the kid must hurdle (e.g. pillows).
- For enlivening, I jump with the kid, even though I am not jumping over anything.

Reverse Spinning ▮▯▯▯▯▯

- Kid holds onto both of your hands behind your back as you spin around.

Similar to **Centrifuge**.

ANTICIPATION:	"Which Hand?", RSG, car engine startup sound
ENLIVENING:	Car SFX (engine, brakes, crash), make up special colors
TENSITY:	Speed, timing of stoplight
UNCERTAINTY:	Stoplight timing/colors, special calls, changing speed
FLUIDITY:	Go until it is too fast for the kid and she falls down, then either restart or transition to another game

FUN	
TIME	
COMPLEXITY	
DANGER	
KID EFFORT	
EXERTION	

MIN AGE:	Toddler
MAX AGE:	School Age
LOCATION:	Any
MATERIALS:	-
PLAYERS:	1-2 kids

CLIMB THE FLAGPOLE IN A TORNADO

Hang on, it's a doozy

PHYSICAL CHALLENGES / CLIMBING / CLIMBING BODY

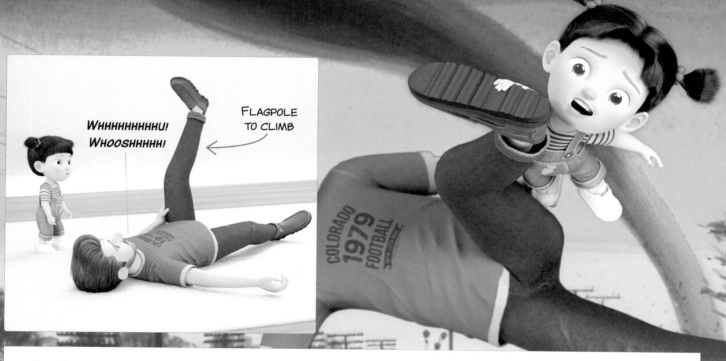

WHHHHHHHHHU! WHOOSHHHHH!

FLAGPOLE TO CLIMB

Description

· Start by lying on your back with one leg in the air. I would also turn on the ceiling fan.
· When the tornado starts, she steps onto you and tries to climb up (and generally hug tightly onto) your leg while you wiggle it around making whoosh sounds until she eventually falls.
· When your leg tires out, you can switch legs by putting the fresh one up up and having her transition over onto that leg.

Similar to:

· BodyBot
· Lifeboat
· Chestboard

ANTICIPATION:	Getting into position, wind sounds
ENLIVENING:	SFX. vicarious exclamations
TENSITY:	Amount of wiggling, speed of movement
UNCERTAINTY:	Randomness of leg movement
FLUIDITY:	Transitions well into other games where you are on your back, like Chestboard or Flipperoo.

FUN	
TIME	
COMPLEXITY	
DANGER	
KID EFFORT	
EXERTION	

MIN AGE:	Toddler
MAX AGE:	Preschooler
LOCATION:	Carpet
MATERIALS:	-
PLAYERS:	1-2 kids

Stairball

Bowling on the staircase

PHYSICAL CHALLENGES / SHOOTING / TARGET PRACTICE

SET UP BOWLING PINS ON THE STAIRCASE.

TAKE TURNS BOWLING DOWN THE STAIRS.

THEN GO DOWNSTAIRS AND THROW THE BALLS AT THE REMAINING PINS.

Description

- Stairball is a mix of bowling and that carnival game where you throw the ball at the milk bottles.
- It works best if the staircase is straight and enclosed (so balls do not go through the railings).
- We would set up the pins randomly (as opposed to in a triangle), spacing them out so you can see things topple over on the way down the stairs.
- Generally, we would not keep score but just take turns, and I would stand farther back to balance the tensity.
- You can use a variety of objects if you do not have toy bowling pins, such as action figures, foam blocks, and even stuff out of the trash can, like empty plastic bottles.

Variation

Block Walls on the Stairs

Superpowers / Destroying

Build foam block castles on the stairs with army guys on top, and then take turns trying to knock the castles down.

ANTICIPATION:	RSG	
ENLIVENING:	SFX (zoom sound when throwing, crash sound when hit, "ent" buzz sound when you miss)	
TENSITY:	Distance from stairs, spacing on stairs, throws per turn	
UNCERTAINTY:	Will it hit the target?	
FLUIDITY:	Have a lot of balls (collecting balls slows things down)	

FUN	
TIME	
COMPLEXITY	
DANGER	
KID EFFORT	
EXERTION	

MIN AGE:	Toddler
MAX AGE:	-
LOCATION:	Stairs
MATERIALS:	Bowling pins, balls
PLAYERS:	1-3 kids

centrifuge

Spin your kid — around and around

PHYSICAL CHALLENGES / HANGING ON / SPINNING

HOLD KID SITTING IN YOUR ARMS

JZUUUUUUUURRRRRRRRRR!

AHHH! HANG ON!

SPIN AROUND IN A TIGHT CIRCLE. AT HIGH SPEED, SLOWING LAY KID OUT FLAT.

Description

- Pretend you are a centrifuge that starts spinning very slowly but gradually accelerates to a high speed.
- Adjust the angle of your arms to keep things interesting.
- Changing directions helps reduce dizziness.
- Depending on the size of the child, it might be easier to hold onto his armpits and shoulders.
- Make sure he knows to tell you if he feels uncomfortable.

Age

Younger kids need to be held onto, while older kids will find it more fun to have the challenge be holding onto you (e.g. Flywheel).

Variations

CENTRIFUGE TUBE
On grass
In a collapsible play tube

- Have kid lie down inside a nylon cylinder tube. pinch the top and bottom sides together (so it is shaped like a "C"), and then pick it up and do Centrifuge.
- He can face in or out, and you can also rotate the tube around while spinning.
- Since you cannot see his face while spinning, it is especially important that he knows to tell you if he becomes uncomfortable.

FLYWHEEL
Toddler to preschool age

- Kid holds onto your forearm with hand on top of hand.
- You spin at increasing speed until kid flies off

Similar to **Traffic Circle**, **Spinning**.

ANTICIPATION:	RSG, machine sounds	
ENLIVENING:	SFX. yelling "Awwww", accelerating crescendo	
TENSITY:	Speed, angle of laying flat or not	
UNCERTAINTY:	Changing speed, direction	
FLUIDITY:	To avoid burnout, only do this a few times before transitioning to something else, like Flips.	

FUN	
TIME	
COMPLEXITY	
DANGER	
KID EFFORT	
EXERTION	

MIN AGE:	Infant
MAX AGE:	Preschooler
LOCATION:	Any
MATERIALS:	-
PLAYERS:	1 kid

59

Sticky Hands
Down low...can't let go!

- This is a short silly one. You will only want to repeat a couple times before it gets too repetitive.
- Once it is time to finish, you can chase the kid with your sticky hands, not being able to let go if you get her.

ANTICIPATION: Put hand out, (generally I run this activity as a surprise)

ENLIVENING: Silly commentary ("Oh my hand, it's so sticky!")

TENSITY: Speed of grasp, duration of hold

UNCERTAINTY: First time: Surprise grasp; subsequent times: Will I get caught?

FLUIDITY: Let go and put your hand back out to start again

PHYSICAL CHALLENGES / EVADING / ESCAPING

SHE TRIES TO SLAP YOUR HAND...

...BUT YOUR HANDS ARE "STICKY"
(YOU GRAB AND HOLD ONTO HER HAND).

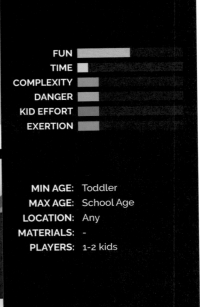

FUN

TIME

COMPLEXITY

DANGER

KID EFFORT

EXERTION

MIN AGE: Toddler
MAX AGE: School Age
LOCATION: Any
MATERIALS: -
PLAYERS: 1-2 kids

EARTHQUAKE
Hang onto dear old dad for dear young life

- Get on your hands and knees with you kid on your back.
- Soft yell "EARTHQUAKE!"
- Slowly start shaking back and forth.
- Increasingly shake/jitter until she falls off.

ANTICIPATION: "EARTHQUAKE!"

ENLIVENING: SFX (crashing sound, rumbling), vicarious exclamations

TENSITY: Speed and amount of shaking, degree of tilt that makes her slide off

UNCERTAINTY: Randomized shaking

FLUIDITY: When she falls, let her climb back up again and restart.

PHYSICAL CHALLENGES / HANGING ON / BOUNCING

EARTHQUAKE!

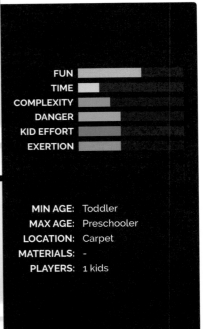

FUN

TIME

COMPLEXITY

DANGER

KID EFFORT

EXERTION

MIN AGE: Toddler
MAX AGE: Preschooler
LOCATION: Carpet
MATERIALS: -
PLAYERS: 1 kids

BODYBOT

Mechanically wielding your kids like a robot

T MINUS 3... 2... 1...

SHE CLIMBS ONTO YOUR LEGS AND WAITS

BEEP... BEEP... CHANGK! ZERKA ZERKA

ACT LIKE A MACHINE, USING HER AS YOUR WORKPIECE

Description

- Start by lying down on your back with your knees up and having her jump up onto your legs.
- Then do a countdown. I use a countdown instead of "Ready, Set, Go" to make it fell more robotic. Make sure to use your robot voice.
- Then move her around (generally using only one axis at a time), so she is lifted in air, flipped around, patted, rolled down your legs, rotated, etc.
- It is fun to have a logical progression by using a theme (like car wash), but most times I'm just stringing together random mechanical motions.
- Eventually resolve into a hug. You can also have her push your nose for powering off/on.
- This game is for small kids; it is impractical with big kids and less fun when they are too tall to rotate around in your arms when holding their hips.

Example Machine Themes

- Car wash (rinse, scrub, suds, rinse, blow dry)
- Massager (squeezes, pokes, rubs, bops, shakes, ...)
- Wind tunnel (flying position, rotate, blow away)
- Package present (put in box, tissue paper, wrap, bow)
- Transformer (mostly just random, but could build car, etc.)

Group Adaptation

You can do this with multiple kids if they take turns.

Similar to **Flipper**

ANTICIPATION:	"T minus 3... 2... 1..."
ENLIVENING:	Robot voice, continuous stream of machine noises
TENSITY:	Speed of operation, how wild the movements are
UNCERTAINTY:	What will the next move be?
FLUIDITY:	End in a hug, and you can either start again or transition to similar games like Chestboard or Flipper.

FUN	
TIME	
COMPLEXITY	
DANGER	
KID EFFORT	
EXERTION	

MIN AGE:	Infant
MAX AGE:	Preschooler
LOCATION:	Carpet
MATERIALS:	-
PLAYERS:	1 kid

PULVERIZER

Endless punches coming your way

- Stand in front of kid and optionally wear padded gloves, hold small pillows, or similar.
- Pretend to punch alternately with each hand in a not-too-fast but powerful sounding way (slow enough she can get out of the way).
- Punch to her sides and pretend you don't notice that she has squirmed away.
- When she calls out and taps you from behind, turn, find her, and repeat.

VARIATIONS
- You must keep your eyes closed.
- **Hulk Punches**
  - One massive punch at a time, Hulk-style.
- **Punch Missiles**
  - No gloves; arm out with pointed knuckles
  - Calibrate aim toward kid like a sentry robot.
  - Fire fist out, and after its impact, repeat.
- **Thor's Hammer**
  - Swing imaginary Mjolnir in the air and have it come smashing down where she was.

BOOM... BOOM...

FUN		
TIME		
COMPLEXITY		
DANGER		
KID EFFORT		
EXERTION		

MIN AGE: Toddler
MAX AGE: School Age
LOCATION: Any
MATERIALS: -
PLAYERS: 1-2 kids

SIMILAR TO: By the Bolts of Zeus

PHYSICAL CHALLENGES / EVADING / DODGING / AVOIDING

Wet Cement

Jump on stepping-stones or get stuck

- Put pillows (stones) across a rug (the cement)
- She tries to get across by only stepping on the stones
- If she steps in the cement, the cement grabs her ankle and holds on until she breaks it off by hitting it with her hammer hands.
- She loses if she falls into the cement.
- Use an area rug with noticeable borders.
- Rearrange the stones each time to make her find different paths across.

ENLIVENING:	SFX (hammer noises, gloop glop sounds), remarks about being stuck in the cement
TENSITY:	Placement of stones (distance, order, quantity), time limit, degree of stepping off that counts as getting stuck
FLUIDITY:	Once across, rearrange the stones for her to cross back on

STONES

CEMENT

FUN		
TIME		
COMPLEXITY		
DANGER		
KID EFFORT		
EXERTION		

MIN AGE: Toddler
MAX AGE: School Age
LOCATION: Carpet
MATERIALS: Couch cushions
PLAYERS: 1-3 kids

LEVELS

1. Big steps to reach stones
2. Jump to reach stones
3. A set path they must follow

PHYSICAL CHALLENGES / JUMPING / LEAPING

FUN	███████
TIME	████
COMPLEXITY	███
DANGER	█████
KID EFFORT	████
EXERTION	██

MIN AGE: Preschooler
MAX AGE: -
LOCATION: Grass or trampoline
MATERIALS: Water hose
PLAYERS: 1-5 kids

TRiPWiRE
Get by unscathed or get blasted

- Turn on the hose and use an attachment that can shoot the water as a straight beam.
- Stand in a grassy area or trampoline and make the water beam a hurdle for the kids to jump over (or roll under) without touching it.
- After they go, they loop around back in line.
- Add some complexity by raising the tripwire's height or moving it around in repeating robotic motions.

PHYSICAL CHALLENGES / JUMPING / HURDLING

FUN	███████
TIME	████
COMPLEXITY	███
DANGER	██████
KID EFFORT	████
EXERTION	███

MIN AGE: Toddler
MAX AGE: -
LOCATION: Trampoline
MATERIALS: -
PLAYERS: 1-3 kids

Stay in the Circle
You had one job: to just stand still

- If your trampoline has a circle painted in the middle, have one kid stay within the circle while the others are trying to bounce her out (but without touching her).
- Standing in the circle is safest, but if the kid rolls up as ball, have her close her mouth so she does not bite her tongue if her knees hit her chin.
- With multiple kids, take turns with one kid in the circle and all the others trying to oust her.

PHYSICAL CHALLENGES / HANGING ON / BALANCING

FUN	███████
TIME	████
COMPLEXITY	████
DANGER	████
KID EFFORT	█████
EXERTION	████

MIN AGE: Preschooler
MAX AGE: School Age
LOCATION: Any
MATERIALS: Item to steal
PLAYERS: 1-2 kids

Statue of Limitations
Be a frozen statue (who chases kids)

- Have a special item (e.g. keys, a lovie).
- Stand in a statue-like pose.
- The kid steals the special item from you.
- The statue breaks out of its stone encasing and chases the kid.
- When you get the item back, return to the original frozen pose (or a new one).

PHYSICAL CHALLENGES / EVADING / ESCAPING

HORSEY

Ride the stallion

- It is a simple pleasure for your kid when she rides on your back like you are a horse.
- Optionally, you can put a rope in your mouth as reins, or let the kid use your hair.

VARIATION
Rodeo
- With kid on your back, spin/rock till she falls
- You can go for time

FUN	
TIME	
COMPLEXITY	
DANGER	
KID EFFORT	
EXERTION	

MIN AGE: Infant
MAX AGE: School Age
LOCATION: Carpet
MATERIALS: -
PLAYERS: 1 kid

PHYSICAL CHALLENGES / HANGING ON / RIDING / BODY

Diaper Bombs

Literally hot, but not literally a potato

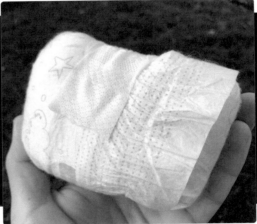

- A tightly rolled up, "used" diaper makes a surprisingly good ball—soft but with heft.
- Throw it to each other, don't let it hit the ground, and toss it back as soon as you can.
- The diaper will start to unravel as you go; you'll need to decide if you will pause the game to fix it or just let things get crazier.
- We liked to play this in a room (sitting backs against the wall), in the trampoline, or long range in the backyard.

FUN	
TIME	
COMPLEXITY	
DANGER	
KID EFFORT	
EXERTION	

MIN AGE: Preschooler
MAX AGE: -
LOCATION: Any
MATERIALS: Wet diaper
PLAYERS: 1-3 kids

PHYSICAL CHALLENGES / CATCHING

My wife does not approve of this game.

Backwards Tag

The blind chase

- You are perpetually "It" as you try to catch the kids.
- You can only move backwards.
- You cannot use your eyes (you don't have to have them closed, but no looking around).
- We always played this on a trampoline with a net cage.

FUN	
TIME	
COMPLEXITY	
DANGER	
KID EFFORT	
EXERTION	

MIN AGE: Toddler
MAX AGE: -
LOCATION: Trampoline
MATERIALS: -
PLAYERS: 1-3 kids

PHYSICAL CHALLENGES / EVADING / BEING PURSUED

FUN	▰▰▰▰▰▰
TIME	▰▰
COMPLEXITY	▰▰▰
DANGER	▰▰▰▰▰▰
KID EFFORT	▰▰▰▰▰
EXERTION	▰▰▰▰▰

MIN AGE: Preschooler
MAX AGE: School Age
LOCATION: Carpet or trampoline
MATERIALS: -
PLAYERS: 1-3 kids

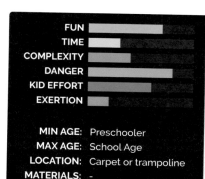

JUMP OVER DADDY
Hurdle me

- Lie down on a soft floor
- Kids stand in a line on the edge of the room.
- One at a time they run up and hurdle over you. You are both frightened and proud.
- To make it more challenging, you can put sofa cushions around you, affecting how high and far they must jump.
- Since it is likely they will occasionally crash, it is safer to do this on a trampoline.

PHYSICAL CHALLENGES / JUMPING / HURDLING

FUN	▰▰▰▰▰
TIME	▰▰▰
COMPLEXITY	▰▰
DANGER	▰▰▰
KID EFFORT	▰▰▰▰
EXERTION	▰▰▰▰

MIN AGE: Toddler
MAX AGE: Preschooler
LOCATION: Any
MATERIALS: -
PLAYERS: 1 kid

CRUSH IM ER
Beware the child compactor

- Start by hugging your child.
- Get a snug grip around him and start repeating "Crush-him" every few seconds in a monotone voice.
- Allow him to make slow yet steady progress; eventually he gets free.
- When playing with one of my daughters, we called this "Crush-her."

PHYSICAL CHALLENGES / EVADING / ESCAPING

FUN	▰▰▰▰▰▰
TIME	▰▰▰
COMPLEXITY	▰▰▰
DANGER	▰▰▰▰
KID EFFORT	▰▰▰
EXERTION	▰▰▰

MIN AGE: Toddler
MAX AGE: School Age
LOCATION: Any
MATERIALS: -
PLAYERS: 1 kid

THE POKE OF DEATH
One jabbing touch is all it takes

- While lying down, taunt kid with a finger hovering above her, pointed at her chest.
- Rapidly reposition a few times, calibrating and giving her time to prepare to block.
- All of the sudden, rapidly bore a hole into her.
- If she blocks you, great, but if not, say in your most distraught voice, "The Poke of Death!"
- You can make this more of a mental challenge by first asking a question and only attacking if she answers incorrectly.

PHYSICAL CHALLENGES / EVADING / DODGING / BLOCKING

MENTAL CHALLENGES

IMPROV
- Make Me Laugh
- Sing Me a Song
- Call and Response Composition

NOISE MAKING
- Poke Music
- SoundFX
- Obscure Animal Noises

JOKING
- Good News Bad News
- Raise Your Hand If...
- Would You Rather

PERFORMING

BEING TESTED
- The Weevil-Rat-Worm
- Food Guy
- Animal Charades
- Dance Off
- Stunts
- Action Figure Remote Control

DISCOVERING
- Treasure Map Hunt
- Treasure Hunt
- Huckle Buckle
- Hide and Seek
- Lost in Space

ENVISIONING
- Imagine
- Describe the Movie Scene

PRETENDING
- Pegarm
- Puppets
- Feed the Pillow Monster Toys

BUILDING
- Marble Autobahn
- Jengabalocks
- Bath Tubes
- Building Forts
- Name Game

NAMING
- Dino Names
- Name This Landscape
- Rhyme by Association
- Alliteration Station

RHYMING

REMEMBERING
- Name Chain Game

TRICKING
- If by That You Mean

CHAPTER 2
Mental Challenges

Games where the most interesting challenge is more mental than physical

WEEVIL-RAT-WORM

He is unimpressed with wrong answers, *but watch out if you're right.*

WHAT IS THE SQUARE ROOT OF 36?

"AH... UMM..."

HAND HOVERS IN SLOW SIDE-TO-SIDE MOTION, READY TO POUNCE.

"7"

IT IS SORELY UNIMPRESSED WITH HER WRONG ANSWERS.

"NO, WAIT. ...6!"

CORRECT ANSWERS, HOWEVER, BRING IT TO ATTENTION.

WHAT ARE THE FIRST 10 DIGITS OF PI?

ASK THE NEXT QUESTION.

"3.141592654"

IT SMILES...

AHH! IT'S EATING MY FLESH!

AND IT BURROWS INTO HER FLESH.

Description

· We play this at bedtime, when kids are motivated to do anything to stay up a little later.
· Move the head slowing back and forth to simulate it being alive.
· The Weevil-Rat-Worm needs to be impressed to attack, so correctly answering easy warmup questions is not enough.
· The closer they get, the more menacing the Weevil-Rat-Worm becomes (e.g. hand gets closer, sways faster, add sound effects).
· Similarly, incorrect answers put the Weevil Rat Worm to sleep (e.g. hand drops lower down and farther away from kid).

Similar to: **Ejector Seat, The Poke of Death**

Group Adaptation

While we only play this one-on-one, it could be adapted so that the kid who answers correctly first is assailed.

Ages

· For younger kids, you can play this so that a wrong answer triggers the attack, while a right answer spares you.
· For older kids, it is more fun to have the right answer attack and for there to be multiple questions needed before an attack.
· School age seems to be the sweet spot for this game.

ANTICIPATION:	Raising hand into position
ENLIVENING:	SFX (hand swooshes, hissing), taunting animal movements, vicarious commentary ("Oh the agony! It's eating my flesh!")
TENSITY:	Difficulty of questions, number of answers before attack
UNCERTAINTY:	Did I say the right answer? Duration of attack
FLUIDITY:	Hand goes back into position after you briefly but firmly attack

FUN

TIME

COMPLEXITY

DANGER

KID EFFORT

EXERTION

MIN AGE:	Toddler
MAX AGE:	-
LOCATION:	Any, bed
MATERIALS:	-
PLAYERS:	1 kid

FOOD GUY

Feed me a food, any food, and let's see what happens

MENTAL CHALLENGES / PERFORMING

ONE PERSON SITS DOWN AND IS THE FOOD GUY, HANDING OUT RANDOM FOOD.

THE FOOD GUY

BIRDY

EAT THE FOOD AND ACT OUT A SILLY RESPONSE AS YOU RUN AROUND FOR MORE FOOD.

Description

- One kid sits on the side and is the "Food Guy" who pretends to hand out food.
- The rest are bounding in circles around the inside perimeter of the trampoline.
- Each time around, the Food Guy calls out and hands a random food to eat.
- She can also call out some foods in combination: "Cookie with hot sauce on it"
- Certain foods can be agreed upon ahead of time to give you powers or weaknesses (e.g. spicy foods can make you run and scream until you get water or milk, sugary foods can make you extra bouncey for awhile).
- Otherwise, just pretend to eat the food and act out your own silly response, like bouncing, burping, or pursuing the other kids.
- We have only ever played this on the trampoline, but I see no reason it could not be adapted for playing elsewhere.

Levels

- Pretend to eat the food you are given
- Special foods give out powers or weaknesses
- Chase kids when you have a speed superpower, or if they take your favorite food.

Example Responses

- Makes you go fast or slow
- Makes you bounce extra high
- Makes you roll around
- Makes you go backwards
- Makes you sick/burb/dizzy/sleepy

		FUN	
ANTICIPATION:	Start bounding along the perimeter, say your hungry	TIME	
ENLIVENING:	Acting out the eating and post-eating movements	COMPLEXITY	
TENSITY:	Different eating action for each food, speed of chase	DANGER	
UNCERTAINTY:	What food will be next? How will Daddy respond?	KID EFFORT	
FLUIDITY:	Around you go until eventually you "get full" and need to lie down. Take turns being the Food Guy.	EXERTION	

MIN AGE: Toddler
MAX AGE: School Age
LOCATION: Trampoline, Any
MATERIALS: -
PLAYERS: 1-3 kids

FIND THE THINGY IN A DARK ROOM

MENTAL CHALLENGES / DISCOVERING

Description

- We usually play this one at bedtime, as it requires a dark room (the darker the better).
- Start by grabbing a special object or lovie. Show it to her, saying something like: "You see this? Could you find this even if it were lost in space?"
- Then have her wait outside the bedroom (no peeking!) while you hide the object in plain view (i.e. not inside drawers or under sheets).
- Turn off the lights, turn on the flashlight, and watch as she searches for it.
- A smartphone flashlight is handy but will light up a wide area. I prefer a small handheld flashlight, since it only lights up a smaller, specific area.
- If it is too difficult, you can give hints using description ("it is not by the dresser") or proximity (cold/warm/hot).

Group Adaptation

This can be done with multiple children in turns, but it is hard for them not to signal the object when they spot it and it is not their turn.

Variation

Huckle Buckle ▪▫▫▫▫▫

- A variation of a common game I played as a child where, in a well-lit room, you hide a small object and have multiple children search for it.
- The goal is to be the first to find it, and when you do, you sit in the center of the room and say "Huckle Buckle!"
- The game is best played when, after discovering the object, you continue to walk around pretending you are still looking, and thus keeping the actual location a secret from others. Then when you head to the center, others assume it is in the wrong location.

ANTICIPATION:	"You see this? Could you find this even if it were lost in space?"	**FUN**	
ENLIVENING:	Commentary as she searches	**TIME**	
TENSITY:	Obviousness of object location, time limit, hints	**COMPLEXITY**	
UNCERTAINTY:	Location of object	**DANGER**	
FLUIDITY:	Can transition to bedtime, shadow puppets	**KID EFFORT**	
		EXERTION	

MIN AGE:	Preschooler
MAX AGE:	-
LOCATION:	Dark room
MATERIALS:	Flashlight
PLAYERS:	1-2 kids

Treasure Map Hunt

Find the map
to find the treasure

FUN	▰▰▰▰▰
TIME	▰▰▰▰
COMPLEXITY	▰▰▰▰
DANGER	▰▰
KID EFFORT	▰▰▰
EXERTION	▰

MIN AGE: Preschooler
MAX AGE: -
LOCATION: Any
MATERIALS: Map
PLAYERS: 1-2 kids

MENTAL CHALLENGES / DISCOVERING

Preparation

Make a Map
· Draw a good final location for hiding the treasure (like in a closet).
· Then draw simple pictures of several other locations, connecting them with a dotted-line. Don't forget the X at the end.
· Embellish the map with trees, mountains, rivers, and creatures.
· Crinkle the map and tear each location off in an irregular shape.

Plant Clues
· Plant the treasure and hide each map piece in the preceding location.
· Repeat until only the first map piece is left. Double check your work
· Conspicuously put that first map piece where the child will find it.

Group Adaptation
· Children of similar ability can work as a team or take turns.
· Or they can work individually on separate paths or even maps. This is more work, but allows you to balance tensity to each individual.

Age
· An easy version of this for children who can read is just to write out location names on sticky notes and hide them in order.
· But drawings are not just for pre-readers' benefit; they create enlivening and are puzzles for kids to interpret the location you were trying to draw.

FUN	▓▓▓
TIME	▓
COMPLEXITY	▓▓▓▓
DANGER	▓
KID EFFORT	▓
EXERTION	▓▓

MIN AGE: Preschooler
MAX AGE: -
LOCATION: Driving
MATERIALS: -
PLAYERS: Family

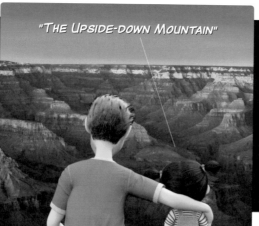

"THE UPSIDE-DOWN MOUNTAIN"

NAME THAT LANDSCAPE

This place should be called...

- This is a brief road trip car game.
- When you enter a new, bizarre, or distinctive landscape, say, "Name that landscape."
- Others need to try to come up with the most creative or funny name for that landscape.

MENTAL CHALLENGES / NAMING

FUN	▓▓▓
TIME	▓▓▓▓
COMPLEXITY	▓▓▓▓▓
DANGER	▓
KID EFFORT	▓▓▓
EXERTION	▓▓

MIN AGE: School Age
MAX AGE: -
LOCATION: Driving
MATERIALS: -
PLAYERS: Family

THIS IS THE PART WHEN THE SPACE CADET THINKS HE IS ALONE ON THE LIFELESS MARTIAN SURFACE WHEN ALL OF THE SUDDEN...

DESCRIBE THE MOVIE SCENE

- While in the car driving on a road trip, turn on some classical background music.
- Based on the music and the current view out the window, tell others to describe a movie scene they can imagine.
- It does not need to be a real movie, we would just make things up.
- For a twist, you can change the station and make her rapidly advance the plot.

MENTAL CHALLENGES / PRETENDING / ENVISIONING

FUN	▓▓▓
TIME	▓▓▓
COMPLEXITY	▓▓▓
DANGER	▏
KID EFFORT	▓▓▓
EXERTION	▓▓

MIN AGE: School Age
MAX AGE: -
LOCATION: Any
MATERIALS: -
PLAYERS: 1-3 kids

BEAGLE
HUSKY
DALMATIAN
WEIMARANER
VIZSLA
XOLOITZCUINTLI
POODLEPOO...

THERE'S NO SUCH THING.

NAME CHAIN GAME

What you said AND this

- Pick a theme (e.g. dog breeds)
- The first person gives and example name (e.g. Poodle")
- The next person repeats that and adds another name ("Poodle, Bulldog")
- Continue taking turns adding on to the name chain until someone cannot do it correctly.
- This does not have to be competitive, you can work together to see how long a chain you can make.

MENTAL CHALLENGES / REMEMBERING

Rhyme by Association

Rhyme...relate...rhyme...relate...

- In this word game, one person rhymes and the other person says related words.
- So the first person says a word, the other person says a rhyming word, then the first says a word associated with it, and on it goes.
- To adjust the tensity you can go for speed or you can allow made up words.

VARIATIONS
- You can do a version where both people do an association (without rhyming).

- **Alliteration Station**
  - Take turns trying to make the longest sentence where each word starts with the same letter.

HOUSE
MOUSE

CHEESE
PLEASE
MANNERS

FUN
TIME
COMPLEXITY
DANGER |
KID EFFORT
EXERTION

MIN AGE: Preschooler
MAX AGE: School Age
LOCATION: Any
MATERIALS: -
PLAYERS: 1 kid

OBSCURE ANIMAL SOUNDS

Verification by absurdly specific precision

- Bedtime with each of my girls has included playing a simple game of "Where's (kid's name)?", where she hides under the covers and I pretend to look for her.
- Obscure Animal Sounds is a funny variation of that, where I am convinced she must have been captured or transformed, and so I try to communicate with her by saying, "Leslie, if you can hear me, make a noise like an (animal) that (overly specific scenario)."
- She then tries to make a noise like that, which is generally hilarious.
- I then reply with a similar pattern, saying something like, "No, that couldn't be her. That sounded more like a (creature) who (overly specific scenario)."
- Then I try again with a new animal noise request.
- I generally end by finding and applauding her.

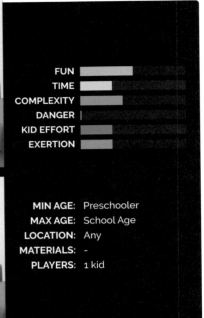

MY DEAR CHILD, IF YOU CAN HEAR ME, MAKE A NOISE LIKE A JOLLY MONKEY WHO HAS JUST FOUND THE SECRET RECIPE FOR MAKING SUPER CHUNKY MONKEY BREAD.

MMHRRRRGAHHH

NO, THAT CAN'T BE HER. THAT SOUNDED MORE LIKE AN ALIEN WHO WAS TRYING TO TELL US THERE IS A TURKEY SANDWICH WAITING FOR US ON THE TABLE.

FUN
TIME
COMPLEXITY
DANGER |
KID EFFORT
EXERTION

MIN AGE: Preschooler
MAX AGE: School Age
LOCATION: Any
MATERIALS: -
PLAYERS: 1 kid

Good News / Bad News
Tell me the good news first.

- In this dinner table game, the kids take turns sharing good news and bad news—generally made up and silly.
- For example, "Hey everybody, I have good news and bad news. The good news is ..."
- It is so basic it is not even a game, but my kid's enjoy coming up with silly dualities.
- Sometime we would do hypothetical tomorrows.

MENTAL CHALLENGES / PERFORMING / JOKING

RAISE YOUR HAND IF...
Who's with me on this?

- A silly dinner table game where one kids surveys the family by saying, "Raise your hand if..." and provides a silly ending like, "...you dream of purple donuts."
- The others either do or don't raise their hands.
- Then it is the next kid's turn.
- While very basic and uninteresting to adults, I have been surprised at how often my younger children love to play this game.

MENTAL CHALLENGES / PERFORMING / JOKING

Would You Rather
Choosing the lesser of two undesireables

- Another common dinner table game.
- One kids says, "Would you rather (scenario 1) or (scenario 2)?"
- The others all chime in with their pick and why.
- Then it is the next kid's turn.
- It is more fun when the scenarios are very bizarre/extreme yet balanced.

Would you rather skydive through clouds made of whipped cream or jump into a pool of Coca-Cola with a swimsuit made of Mentos?

MENTAL CHALLENGES / PERFORMING / JOKING

Action Figure Remote Control
Strike a pose like a hero

- Hold up a stuffed animal, a doll, or a large action figure.
- Put the figure into a specific pose (e.g. arms wide).
- The child needs to match and hold that position.
- Update the figure's pose as the child quickly matches it.

MENTAL CHALLENGES / PERFORMING

FUN	▰▰▰
TIME	▰▰
COMPLEXITY	▰▰
DANGER	▏
KID EFFORT	▰▰
EXERTION	▰

MIN AGE: Preschooler
MAX AGE: -
LOCATION: Any
MATERIALS: -
PLAYERS: Family

ANT
BEE
CAT
DOG
ELEPHANT
FISH
GOAT
HIPPO
IGUANA
JELLYFISH
KANGAROO
LION
MOOSE
...

Name Game
A name by any other letter will not do

- This is a simple dinner table game with lots of variations. A kid says the first letter of a name he is thinking of and everyone else guesses.
- You can go around in a circle or have the person who guessed correctly go next.
- One variation was to go through the alphabet on a subject (e.g. animals, Bible names).

MENTAL CHALLENGES / NAMING

MAKE ME LAUGH
Easier done than said

- This is a dinner table game we would play where one person says "Make me laugh," and each person at the table goes in turn trying to make him laugh.
- But as soon as he laughs, the turn is over and the next person says "Make me laugh," and it goes around again.
- This can get silly fast, so consider adding some boundaries ahead of time.

FUN	
TIME	
COMPLEXITY	
DANGER	
KID EFFORT	
EXERTION	

MIN AGE:	Preschooler
MAX AGE:	School Age
LOCATION:	Any
MATERIALS:	-
PLAYERS:	Family

MENTAL CHALLENGES / PERFORMING / IMPROV

If by that you mean...
Only on opposite day

- Kid asks you to do something
  - e.g. pick me up
- You say: "Alright, if by ___ you mean ___" and do something totally different or the opposite
  - e.g. tickle her feet
- Repeat
- At a comic moment when kid asks for the opposite of what she actually wants, just say "OK" and do it

FUN	
TIME	
COMPLEXITY	
DANGER	
KID EFFORT	
EXERTION	

MIN AGE:	Toddler
MAX AGE:	School Age
LOCATION:	Any
MATERIALS:	-
PLAYERS:	1-2 kids

MENTAL CHALLENGES / TRICKING

STUNTS
Oh yeah? Match this!

- On the trampoline, one person does a stunt, then the others take turns trying to recreate it.
- While not their turn, players should sit at edge and can also clap, heckle, cheer, etc.
- Add difficulty by having to combine each one.

VARIATION: Dance Off
Each person gets about 30 seconds to dance their heart out in the center of the trampoline while the others clap out the beat and cheer.

FUN	
TIME	
COMPLEXITY	
DANGER	
KID EFFORT	
EXERTION	

MIN AGE:	Preschooler
MAX AGE:	-
LOCATION:	Trampoline
MATERIALS:	-
PLAYERS:	1-5 kids

MENTAL CHALLENGES / PERFORMING

FUN	▓▓▓▓
TIME	▓▓
COMPLEXITY	▓▓▓
DANGER	▏
KID EFFORT	▓▓
EXERTION	▓▓▓

MIN AGE: Toddler
MAX AGE: -
LOCATION: Any
MATERIALS: -
PLAYERS: 1 kid

CALL & RESPONSE COMPOSITION
Do be do be do

- Make an acapella song together by taking turns kicking variations of a riff back and forth.
- For us this was a mixture of scat talk and basic classical theme/variation.
- Don't be afraid to overlap each other.
- For conclusion or for special effect, join in and do a duet.

MENTAL CHALLENGES / PERFORMING / IMPROV

FUN	▓▓▓▓▓
TIME	▓▓▓▓
COMPLEXITY	▓▓▓
DANGER	▓
KID EFFORT	▓▓▓
EXERTION	▓▓▓

MIN AGE: Preschooler
MAX AGE: -
LOCATION: Any
MATERIALS: -
PLAYERS: Family

Sing Me a Song
Seriously, like, right now

- This is a game we would play at the dinner table as a family.
- Given 2 or 3 random things, take turns where each person makes up and sings a little ditty that involves those things.
- The goal is not so much to compete against each other but to all give it a try.
- If you struggle with this type of thing:
  - use the melody of a familiar song
  - try using limericks or simple couplets

MENTAL CHALLENGES / PERFORMING / IMPROV

Poke Music
Can you feel it?

- At its most basic level, you just take turns poking each other all over, making a different sound for each spot, generally musical, like finger scales.
- You can switch up who makes the noise (i.e. poker or pokee)
- Usually I would pretend the kid is a full-body musical instrument, and I could change instruments when needed.
- Sometime I used a wand, like a pencil with a big eraser, to do the tapping, but when you are jamming a funky groove, fingers are unmatched.

MENTAL CHALLENGES / PERFORMING / NOISE MAKING

SOUNDFX
That sounds like...

- Start by making an interesting sound.
- Then he says, "That sounds like..." and describes it.
- Then he makes a sound and it is your turn to describe it.
- The sounds start as short sound effects but progressively become longer and sillier combinations; likewise, the descriptions eventually become mini-stories.
- Short, obvious answers ("that sounds like a scream") are less interesting than elaborate, wackier ones ("that sounds like what the germs say when you wash your hands").

MENTAL CHALLENGES / PERFORMING / NOISE MAKING

77

BATTLES

RACING
- Chase at Light Switch
- Race Up the Mountain
- Battleball

WRESTLING
- AT-AT Attack
- Wrestle to Kiss
- GoGo Juice

TRIPPING
- No Arm Knockdown

KICKING
- TowardKick
- Balloon Soccer
- Trampoline Soccer

CRASHING
- Run and Crash
- Rockpile
- Storm the Castle
- Juggernaut

MARTIAL ARTS
- Ninjaballoon
- Krazy-Fu

BOXING
- Kitchen Bottle Punchout
- Balloon Belly Punchout
- Balloon Fist Bombs

FIGHTING

SWORD PLAY
- Steal Sword from Pirate
- Pillow Knockdown
- Bo Fighting
- Sword Fighting

COMBAT
- Stuffed Animal Artillary
- Marshmallow Games
- Marble Crossfire
- Bunkbed Battleship
- Crib Wars
- Robot Must Destroy
- Throw a Balloon at the Giant
- Boss Level
- Tableball

CHAPTER 3
Battles

Competitive games and contests with the goal of overcoming the opponent

- Generally head-to-head duels (not turn-taking)
- A struggle for victory, though generally not a prize

Trampoline Soccer
Close range goal-making

BATTLES / KICKING

ASSIGN GOALS USING THE POLES THAT HOLD UP THE NET.

PLAY SIMPLIFIED SOCCER WITHOUT USING YOUR HANDS.

Description

- We always played this in a trampoline with a net, which makes the gameplay more "arena-style."
- This is a fast, high-scoring game. We usually played to 11 before starting a new game.
- Be decisive on whether something is a goal or not. I am usually very generous in the kid's favor.
- We preferred a softer, bigger ball, which is safer too.

Group Adaptation

This game is likely too crowded for group play. We only ever played this one-on-one.

Variations

Balloon Soccer
- Play soccer with balloons. It is even better if there are several of them.
- This is safe enough to play indoors. We use couches, chairs and walls for goals.
- I generally only play with one kid at a time.

Hallway Soccer
- In a hallway, establish opposing walls or thresholds as goals.
- Use a small stuffed toy soccer ball. Bigger ones result in fewer points, more predictable gameplay, and more potential damage.

ANTICIPATION:	RSG
ENLIVENING:	Smack talk
TENSITY:	Deciding if a goal or not, allowing kid to use hands
UNCERTAINTY:	Where the ball goes when you kick it
FLUIDITY:	Keep shots low for safety and because it takes time to reestablish gameplay when the ball goes out.

FUN	
TIME	
COMPLEXITY	
DANGER	
KID EFFORT	
EXERTION	

MIN AGE:	Preschooler
MAX AGE:	-
LOCATION:	Trampoline
MATERIALS:	Soccer ball
PLAYERS:	1 kid

JUGGERNAUT

HEAD-ON PILLOW CRASHING

READY... SET... GO!

HOLD CUSHIONS TO YOUR CHESTS

CRASH!

RUN/WADDLE TOWARDS EACH OTHER

JUGGERNAUT

FALL BACK AND SAY "JUGGERNAUT"

REPEAT

Description

- You could easily knock them over if you tried, so this game is more about letting them win most of the time without them realizing it's rigged.
- I do not play this with any fighting elements to it, as they tend to get boring or frustrating for the kid. I generally just crash and fall down, and then rapidly repeat.
- When letting the child win, I hold onto him as I slowly tumble backwards.

Age & Group Adaptation

- With multiple kids, I have them form a line at the start position and go in turn.
- Young ones do not have to carry a cushion.

Variation

THE JUGGERNAUT WALL

- No cushions. Instead, you hold up an air mattress vertically in the middle of a room as a wall they run into and try to knock over.
- Be prepared for the young ones to go flying back; spread out some pillows or blankets on the ground, or at a minimum play on carpet.

ANTICIPATION:	RSG, "Get in position"
ENLIVENING:	SFX (battle cry), Braveheart speech
TENSITY:	Ease of knocking you over
UNCERTAINTY:	Who will get knocked over?
FLUIDITY:	After you say "Juggernaut" say "get in position" to restart

FUN	
TIME	
COMPLEXITY	
DANGER	
KID EFFORT	

MIN AGE:	Toddler
MAX AGE:	-
LOCATION:	Carpet
MATERIALS:	Cushions
PLAYERS:	1-2 kids

KRAZY-FU

Do you know Krazy-fu? Neither do I.

Do you know Krazy-Fu?

THEN FLAIL YOUR ARMS IN THE MOST RIDICULOUS MANNER POSSIBLE.

Description

- Start by striking a martial arts pose and asking, "Do you know Krazy-fu?"
- After a dramatic pause, slowly pursue kid while hands are flailing in the most ridiculous manner possible.
- The rest is up to you. Just do not actual beat up your child.
- This is not a game that lasts very long or repeats much. It is mostly used to get a laugh or begin a chase.

Levels

I've only done this with one kid at a time. I imagine you would get beat up if there were multiple krazy-fu artists attacking you.

ANTICIPATION:	Assuming position, saying "Do you know Krazy-fu?"	
ENLIVENING:	SFX and how extremely you "flail"	
TENSITY:	How close you come to actually making contact, avoiding attacks	
UNCERTAINTY:	Almost random attack motions	
FLUIDITY:	Can transition to DodgeArm or similar	

FUN	
TIME	
COMPLEXITY	
DANGER	
KID EFFORT	
EXERTION	

MIN AGE:	Toddler
MAX AGE:	-
LOCATION:	Any
MATERIALS:	-
PLAYERS:	1 kid

STORM THE CASTLE

JUMP INTO THE FRAY WITH RECKLESS ABANDON

BATTLE / CRASHING

Description

- Start by lying on a carpeted floor with lots of cushions and pillows on and around you.
- Kids line up on the other side of the room and take turns running up and jumping onto you.
- Generally they will land on the cushion on your chest, but you will need to anticipate and make sure they always have a safe landing.
- Once on top of you, gracefully slide her off to the ground and reset.

Group Adaptation

For everyone's safety, I generally have the kids go one at a time.

Similar to

The Wave, Lifeboat, Magic Cusion Ride

Variations

There are lots of potential variations of this game just by changing the theme. For example, instead of a castle, "Cowabunga" enacts a run and surf idea and "Rockpile" a street fight theme.

Cowabunga

- They each have to yell out a word as they run up
- If it is a cool word like "Cowabunga", they get to surf for a bit on the cushion before landing.
- Poor word choices, such as potty talk will get them rejected.

ROCKPILE

- Similar setup, but the kids are trying to attack you.
- You throw insults like "Next!", "Eat more fatty foods", etc.

ANTICIPATION:	RSG, "Get in position"	**FUN**	**MIN AGE**:	Toddler
ENLIVENING:	SFX (crashing), taunting	**TIME**	**MAX AGE**:	-
TENSITY:	Rejecting (i.e. deflecting them instead of a nice landing)	**COMPLEXITY**	**LOCATION**:	Carpet
UNCERTAINTY:	Will I get rejected? Will I fall?	**DANGER**	**MATERIALS**:	Cushions
FLUIDITY:	Cycle kids back to starting point before the next iteration	**KID EFFORT**	**PLAYERS**:	1-2 kids

CRIBWARS

Jettison all the stuffed animals!

BATTLES / COMBAT

Description

- Young children somehow accumulate lots of stuffed animals. The smaller the stuffed animals are, the better they are for this game.
- In this game you try to throw all the stuffed animals into the crib, while he tries to throw them out of the crib.
- Cribs work perfectly for being a big basket to shoot into (beds and sofas, not so much).
- We generally play this without actually throwing the stuffed animals at the person, but that is fun too, so long as no one gets hurt.

Age

- Kids age out of cribs before they age out of this game.
- For older kids, you can play on a bunkbed, if you have one.

Variation

In bathtub with beach balls

Similar to

Bunkbed Battleship

ANTICIPATION:	RSG
ENLIVENING:	SFX (shooting/throwing, getting hit)
TENSITY:	Frequency of throwing
UNCERTAINTY:	Randomizing target and frequency
FLUIDITY:	The game can go on forever if you let it, but generally I try to win so the room is clean

- FUN
- TIME
- COMPLEXITY
- DANGER
- KID EFFORT
- EXERTION

MIN AGE:	Infant
MAX AGE:	Toddler
LOCATION:	Crib
MATERIALS:	Stuffed animals
PLAYERS:	1 kid

BUNKBED BATTLESHIP
Aiming for the unseen target

BATTLE / COMBAT

MISS!

OH! YOU HIT MY FACE!

COLORADO 1979 FOOTBALL

Description
- Each person should stay still for the duration of the game, and no peeking.
- Take turns (instead of rapid fire), so that the game is about calibration and aim.
- If the game is too easy for you, you can make it more challenging by having multiple items that you need to hit (e.g. pillow, stuffed animal), while the kid only needs to hit you. Alternatively, you could allow the kid to move between turns.
- You can use stuffed animals for this game instead of balls.
- This definitely works best with a bunk bed; however, you could play this in other places so long as neither person can see the other (e.g. across a room with a sofa in the middle).

Similar to
- Crib Wars, Battle Ball

	Kid	Adult
Expectation	Try to throw the ball at Daddy before he hits you	Try to throw the ball at the kid before she hits you
Challenge	Cannot see Daddy	Cannot see her, and sometimes she moves
Fulfillment	Hitting Daddy in the face and not getting in trouble	Executing laser-like precision to sink her

ANTICIPATION:	RSG	**FUN**	
ENLIVENING:	SFX (shooting, ball falling, crash)	**TIME**	
TENSITY:	Having multiple items to hit, allowing kid to move between turns	**COMPLEXITY**	
		DANGER	
UNCERTAINTY:	When will I get hit?	**KID EFFORT**	
FLUIDITY:	Can transition to bedtime or Weevil-Rat-Worm	**EXERTION**	

MIN AGE:	Toddler
MAX AGE:	School Age
LOCATION:	Bed
MATERIALS:	Balls
PLAYERS:	1 kid

BATTLE BALL

Aim. Fire. Repeat.

- You need lots of play gym balls.
- The main objective is to throw the balls at each other, usually with furniture barricades and couch cushion shields.
- A variation we liked was to have your hands pretend to be a UFO, and they need to hit it out of the sky.

ANTICIPATION: RSG

ENLIVENING: Excessive theatrics when hit

TENSITY: Speed of throw, distance apart

UNCERTAINTY: Curvature of ball flight, make sure to throw from far enough away that they can avoid getting hit

FLUIDITY: Transitions well into Shoops for cleanup

BATTLES / COMBAT

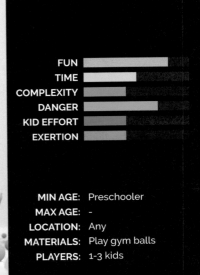

FUN	
TIME	
COMPLEXITY	
DANGER	
KID EFFORT	
EXERTION	

MIN AGE: Preschooler
MAX AGE: -
LOCATION: Any
MATERIALS: Play gym balls
PLAYERS: 1-3 kids

NO ARM KNOCKDOWN

Trip or be tripped

- With your arms behind your back, try to make others fall by tripping them.
- We have only done this on a trampoline, but it might work well in a inflatable bouncy house.
- A fun variation we liked is for you to try this on your back while they are running around.

ANTICIPATION: RSG

ENLIVENING: Smack talk

TENSITY: Speed, how aggressive you attack, allowing them to use their hands

UNCERTAINTY: Will they fall or not, timing of your attacks

FLUIDITY: Players can get up right away and continue playing

BATTLES / TRIPPING

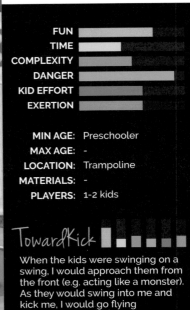

FUN	
TIME	
COMPLEXITY	
DANGER	
KID EFFORT	
EXERTION	

MIN AGE: Preschooler
MAX AGE: -
LOCATION: Trampoline
MATERIALS: -
PLAYERS: 1-2 kids

TowardKick

When the kids were swinging on a swing, I would approach them from the front (e.g. acting like a monster). As they would swing into me and kick me, I would go flying backwards (and push them higher).

NINJABALLOON

Attack the balloon like a ninja master, just don't let it touch the ground

STRIKE A MARTIAL ARTS POSE AND TOSS A BALLOON IN THE AIR.

TAKE TURNS USING "KARATE" MOVES TO KNOCK IT AWAY, NOT LETTING IT TOUCH THE FLOOR.

Description

- The objective is to take turns hitting it and to not be the one who lets it hit the ground.
- Slicing with a flat hand and punching with a fist are the easiest moves to use; kicking is more challenging.
- It is fun to use a helium latex balloon that has lost some of its buoyancy and just barely sinks. Mylar balloon can be used, but are a lot noisier.

Similar to

Balloon Belly Punchout, Krazy-Fu

Group Adaptation

For everyone's safety, I generally have the kids go one at a time.

Variation

The kid can play this solo, with you as an officiator counting how many hits in a row she can do.

ANTICIPATION:	Strike a martial arts pose, RSG	**MIN AGE**:	Toddler
ENLIVENING:	SFX (martial arts fighting sounds)	**MAX AGE**:	-
TENSITY:	Location you send the balloon back to, speed	**LOCATION**:	Any
UNCERTAINTY:	Balloon location	**MATERIALS**:	Balloon
FLUIDITY:	Transitions well into Krazy-fu	**PLAYERS**:	1-3 kids

FUN
TIME
COMPLEXITY
DANGER
KID EFFORT
EXERTION

BOSS LEVEL
If life is a video game, I'm the boss

- In this game we do a battle pretending to be in a video game, with me being the boss.
- She has a pillow for a sword and another for a shield.
- Slowly pursue her and exaggerate the effects of her attacks.
- If you capture her, make a sad computer sound, say "Game over," and restart the level.
- If she wins, say "You win!" with happy SFX.

BATTLES / COMBAT

FUN	
TIME	
COMPLEXITY	
DANGER	
KID EFFORT	
EXERTION	

MIN AGE: Toddler
MAX AGE: School Age
LOCATION: Any
MATERIALS: Pillows
PLAYERS: 1 kid

BALLOON BELLY PUNCHOUT
Punch the balloon-belly

- Put a balloon under your shirt like a big belly
- The kid can only hit you in the balloon.
- You can play where the kid has a balloon too, but I found the height differences make this too difficult unless you are on your knees.
- Make sure to bounce way back every time they hit you and to come lumbering toward them in a silly, slow way.

BATTLES / FIGHTING / BOXING

Variations

BALLOON FIST BOMBS

- In this version, you each have balloons in your hands and you punch each other in the face.
- To make it more challenging, try to avoid getting hit while not moving your feet.

Throw a Balloon at the Giant

- You approach slowly but thunderingly
- They throw a balloon at you
- The balloon has an exaggerated effect of knocking you back each time

FUN	
TIME	
COMPLEXITY	
DANGER	
KID EFFORT	
EXERTION	

MIN AGE: Toddler
MAX AGE: School Age
LOCATION: Any
MATERIALS: Balloon
PLAYERS: 1-2 kids

Robot must destroy
Robot must destroy the boy, so turn it off

- In this game, they would put a mask on me, which turned me into a robot bent on catching and destroying them.
- I would say: "Robot must destroy the boy" as I slowly pursued them, walking around mechanically on my knees.
- Meanwhile, they would climb all over me, and if they pulled the mask off, I'd say "powering down," and fall to the ground;

BATTLES / COMBAT

MARSHMALLOW GAMES
Quite possibly the ultimate material

- You'll need to go to the grocery store and get the jumbo sized marshmallows (they are about 2 inches long)
- We would play a whole variety of games with them, including:
  - Catch
  - Battle Ball / DodgeMarshmellow
  - Shoops
  - Tennis, Baseball, and more

VARIOUS

GOGO JUICE

Slowmo wrestling...until you use the juice

BATTLE / WRESTLING

MUST...
DRINK...
GOGO JUICE

Description

- It is important to have a defined play area with a boundary. Kneel on all fours on an area rug or similar.
- Wrestle the kids, who can move freely in the playing area.
- You, however, can only move in slow motion and have to stay on your knees (so that you are approachable for tackling).
- In times of desperation, say "Must… drink… GoGo Juice" and pretend to open a can and drink it. Then you can move very quickly to capture and tickle them. The GoGo juice wears off after about 5-10 seconds.
- There is no medium speed for you in this game, only slow and really fast.

	Kid	Adult
Expectation	Wrestle with a slower version of Daddy	Wrestle with kids
Challenge	Daddy can sometimes "go fast"	Kids will pile on you
Fulfillment	Ticklekissed by Daddy	Briefly having superpowers

ANTICIPATION:	RSG, introduce juice each time with "Must… drink… GoGo juice…"	**FUN**	**MIN AGE:** Toddler
ENLIVENING:	SFX, slow motion, opening/drinking juice, moving extra fast	**TIME**	**MAX AGE:** -
TENSITY:	Ease of tackling you, speed of movements	**COMPLEXITY**	**LOCATION:** Carpet
UNCERTAINTY:	When you will use GoGo juice	**DANGER**	**MATERIALS:** -
FLUIDITY:	After you capture them, you run out of GoGo juice, they escape, and you restart.	**KID EFFORT**	**PLAYERS:** 1-3 kids
		EXERTION	

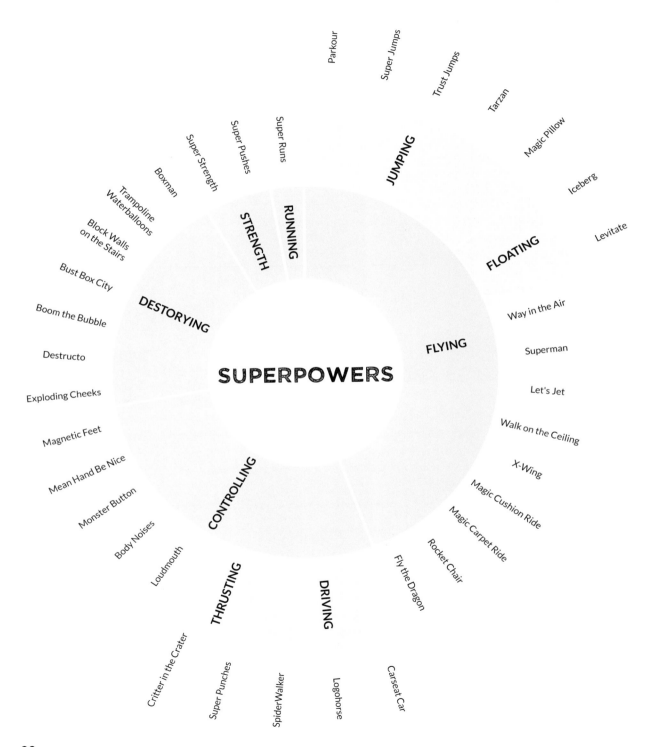

SUPERPOWERS

JUMPING
Parkour
Super Jumps
Trust Jumps

FLOATING
Tarzan
Magic Pillow
Iceberg
Levitate

FLYING
Way in the Air
Superman
Let's Jet
Walk on the Ceiling
X-Wing
Magic Cushion Ride
Magic Carpet Ride
Rocket Chair
Fly the Dragon

DRIVING
Carseat Car
Logohorse

THRUSTING
SpiderWalker
Super Punches
Critter in the Crater

CONTROLLING
Loudmouth
Body Noises
Monster Button
Mean Hand Be Nice

DESTORYING
Magnetic Feet
Exploding Cheeks
Destructo
Boom the Bubble
Bust Box City
Block Walls on the Stairs
Waterballoons
Trampoline
Boxman

STRENGTH
Super Strength
Super Pushes

RUNNING
Super Runs

CHAPTER 4

Superpowers

Activities where you augment the child's capabilities in a fantastic way, such as by removing limitations or amplifying current capabilities.

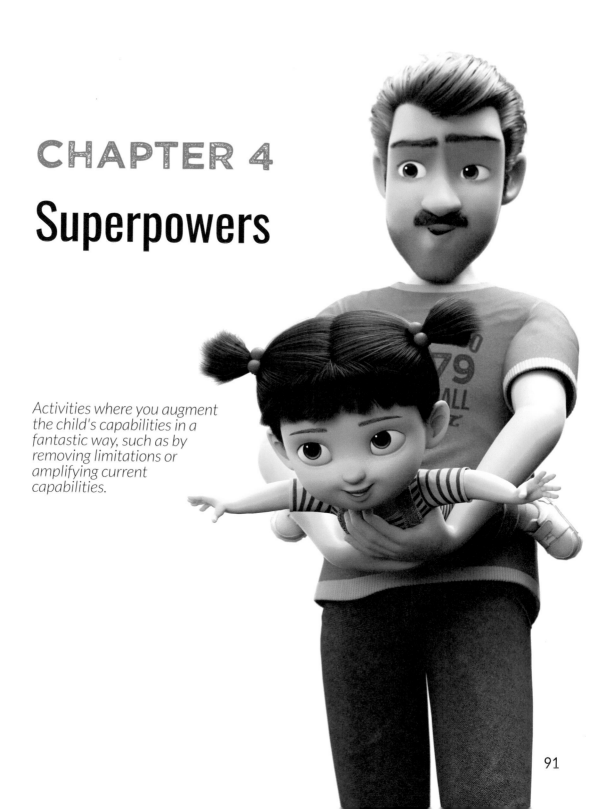

PARKOUR

There are no limits. So... sure. Why not? Let's do it.

SUPERPOWERS / RUNNING

SLIDE DOWN THE STAIR BANISTER!

JUMP ONTO OR OVER THINGS!

RUN ALONG THE TOP OF THE COUCH!

DIVE AND ROLL UNTO THE COUCH!

JUMP OFF OF WALLS!

ANTICIPATION:	RSG	**MIN AGE:**	Infant
ENLIVENING:	SFX, commentary, vicarious exclamations	**MAX AGE:**	School Age
TENSITY:	Effort the kid must provide, allowing "fails" and redos	**LOCATION:**	Any
UNCERTAINTY:	What's next? Will I make it?	**MATERIALS:**	-
FLUIDITY:	You will tire quickly, so plan your transition early	**PLAYERS:**	1 kid

FUN
TIME
COMPLEXITY
DANGER
KID EFFORT
EXERTION

Description

- This adaptation of freestyle street running is probably our favorite superpower activity, mostly because you can do it almost anywhere and it is different every time.
- Your main role is to make it a lot safer for your kid's to do amazing stunts.
- But you are also a director, calling out the next move so you are both working towards the same goal.

Example Run (Basic)

- Run and jump onto couch
- Run across couch and jump onto arm chair
- Jump off of wall and land back onto couch

Example Run (Advanced)

- Run up and do a monkey vault over the ottoman
- Run at wall and do a wall flip, landing on couch arm
- Skip on couch cushions and precision jump onto arm chair
- Precision jump to piano bench and (gently) play piano with toes
- Precision jump or cat leap to window sill
- Balance along window sill, cat leaping so she is hanging onto fireplace mantle
- Shimmy along mantle, bound across to kitchen (perhaps rolling or bear crawling across carpet)
- Vault onto kitchen table
- Run along edge, precision jump to kitchen counter, then to kitchen island counter
- Bound on each barstool and forward flip down
- Run across room and get thrown from a distance onto couch

Group Adaptation

Since you can only do this with one child at a time, other children will have to wait for their turns.

Age

- Obviously the smaller the child, the easier it will be to lift and maneuver her (and the more magical it will seem to her).
- As they age though, you can make them do more of the exertion and directing while you function more as a safety guide and encourager.

Similar to; Super Jumps, Super Runs, Walk on the Ceiling

SPIDER WALKER
Command your robot spider ——— and it will take you places ———

SUPERPOWERS / CONTROLLING / DRIVING

Description

- Start by getting in a "crab walking" position and have the child climb into your lap, holding onto your knees.
- For the little kids, you can just "walk" the spider around. I make things get increasingly unstable as I go, until they eventually fall off.
- As they get older, you can let her direct where to go by giving pre-defined commands or make you move by pointing.
  - For example, "Forward" and "Backward" make you move one unit, while "Left" and "Right" only make you turn 45 degrees in that direction.

Variations

- She must give a command and an amount ('forward 3')
- She must give a series of commands up front. When you crash into a wall, have her give you another set of commands.
- You can have a consequence from invalid command (sound, shake, collapse, etc.)

LOGOHORSE ■■■■■■

- Have kid climb on your back direct you around
- Also see **Horsey**, a simpler variation.

ANTICIPATION:	"What is your command?" in robot voice		
ENLIVENING:	SFX (robotics, beep/shake/collapse on failure)		
TENSITY:	Commands (number, accuracy), grace amount		
UNCERTAINTY:	Did I calculate it correctly?		
FLUIDITY:	You can use your robot voice to give hints like available commands and where to go.		

FUN ▬▬▬▬▬
TIME ▬▬▬
COMPLEXITY ▬▬▬
DANGER ▬▬▬
KID EFFORT ▬▬▬▬
EXERTION ▬▬▬▬

MIN AGE: Infant
MAX AGE: Preschooler
LOCATION: Any
MATERIALS: -
PLAYERS: 1 kid

FUN	
TIME	
COMPLEXITY	
DANGER	
KID EFFORT	
EXERTION	

MIN AGE:	Preschooler
MAX AGE:	School Age
LOCATION:	Any
MATERIALS:	-
PLAYERS:	1 kid

SUPER STRENGTH
See, I told you broccoli makes you strong

- Occasionally when a child holds onto your leg, she will try to lift you up—let her.
- You'll need to stand up high on your other leg's toes. Make it look like you're hips are going up, and wave your arms like all of the sudden you are only being held up by her.
- This works as a nice introduction to similar activities, such as Super Pushes, or to battles, such as Boss Level.

SUPERPOWERS / STRENGTH

FUN	
TIME	
COMPLEXITY	
DANGER	
KID EFFORT	
EXERTION	

MIN AGE:	Toddler
MAX AGE:	Preschooler
LOCATION:	Any
MATERIALS:	-
PLAYERS:	1 kid

Super Pushes
I'm such a pushover

- This is essentially a battle game where you are mock fighting, but you can only push each other.
- Since she is super strong, you go flying each time she pushes you.
- Exaggeration here is the key to making this fun for her and not short-lived.
- A variation of this is **Super Punches**.
- Another variation is moving you without touching you (i.e. **the Force**).

SUPERPOWERS / STRENGTH

FUN	
TIME	
COMPLEXITY	
DANGER	
KID EFFORT	
EXERTION	

MIN AGE:	Infant
MAX AGE:	Toddler
LOCATION:	Any
MATERIALS:	-
PLAYERS:	1 kid

SUPER JUMPS
Of course you can make it from here

- Decide together on what would be an amazing thing to jump over or onto.
- Holding both her hands, do a "Ready...set...go" and as she jumps, lift her the rest of the way.
- This can be done on stairs, over railings, and onto ledges, and is handy when waiting in line.
- The next level is to toss her onto a bed or soft couch from a distance.

SUPERPOWERS / FLYING / JUMPING

MONSTER BUTTON

Find the button that unleashes the beast

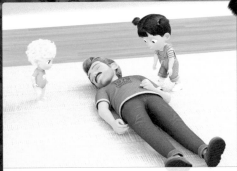

A SPECIFIC SPOT ON YOUR BODY CAN WAKE YOU.

KIDS POKE YOU UNTIL THEY FIND IT.

WHEN THEY DO, JUMP UP WITH A LOUD ROAR, CHASE THEM, CAPTURE THEM, AND KISS THEM.

Description

- If you prefer, the button does not have to be on your body; it can be anywhere in the room. Kids do enjoy poking you and sticking their fingers up your nose, though.
- I clarify ahead of time that it is not under my eyelids and nowhere near my privates.
- If there are multiple kids, prepare to be abused.

Variation

BODY NOISES

- Kid pushes any area of my body like a button, you make a unique noise for each spot.
- Remember to make the same sound each time they touch the same spot.

Levels

1. Single button reanimates you
2. Multiple buttons, each making you do different things
3. Remote control buttons (ones not on your body)

Similar to

- Statue of Limitations
- Poke Music
- The Poke of Death

	Kid	Adult
Expectation	Poke Daddy	Getting poked like a pin cushion
Challenge	Being chased	Devising (and remembering) actions for each button
Fulfillment	Getting caught and kissed	Chasing laughing kids

ANTICIPATION:	Lying in position
ENLIVENING:	SFX (roaring to life, motion sounds), speed of reanimation (fast surprise or slow buildup)
TENSITY:	Specificity of button location
UNCERTAINTY:	Random button location so they wonder, "Is this it?"
FLUIDITY:	Re-pushing button can reset you back to sleep

- FUN
- TIME
- COMPLEXITY
- DANGER
- KID EFFORT
- EXERTION

MIN AGE:	Toddler
MAX AGE:	School Age
LOCATION:	Any
MATERIALS:	-
PLAYERS:	1-3 kids

CARSEAT CAR

He's already buckled up, so let him drive

- This is for when you are sitting down waiting somewhere, and the baby is strapped in the carseat on the ground by your feet (and especially if he is getting fussy).
- Put your toes under the front edges of the carseat to lift it up slightly, tilting it left or right to simulate a car making sharp turns. You might need to hold onto the top handlebar.
- We had a toy dangling down from the handlebar, which the baby could hold onto and "steer" with.

SUPERPOWERS / CONTROLLING / DRIVING

Fly the Dragon

Everyone should have a good luck dragon

- One of the ways I would get my kids up to bed was to pretend to be a dragon they could fly on.
- The kid climbs on your back and you fly him up to bed, flapping your arms like wings.
- Similar to **Let's Jet** and **Superman**.

SUPERPOWERS / FLYING

FUN	▇▇▇▇▇▇▇▇
TIME	▇▇
COMPLEXITY	▇▇▇
DANGER	▇▇▇▇
KID EFFORT	▇▇▇▇▇
EXERTION	▇▇▇▇▇▇

MIN AGE: Toddler
MAX AGE: Preschooler
LOCATION: Any
MATERIALS: -
PLAYERS: 1 kid

SUPERMAN
Soar up and fly away

- At the bottom of the stairs, have her interlace her fingers around your right hand's palm while you say: "It's a bird, it's a plane, it's..."
- "...Superman!" Lift her straight up toward the ceiling, then over onto your shoulder and run up the stairs and around the house, resting her down gently on a bed.
- Young kids have no idea who Superman is and have hilarious answers to "It's a bird, it's a plane, it's...", like: "It's a bird." "It's in the sky."

SUPERPOWERS / FLYING

FUN	▇▇▇▇▇
TIME	▇▇
COMPLEXITY	▇▇
DANGER	▇▇
KID EFFORT	▇▇▇▇▇
EXERTION	▇▇▇

MIN AGE: Infant
MAX AGE: Infant
LOCATION: Any
MATERIALS: -
PLAYERS: 1 kid

MAGNETIC FEET
I've got your feet on my mind

- This is an activity for after a diaper change.
- Hold his ankles and press his feet against your forehead.
- Your head is stuck to the soles of his feet, and he has to kick or pry them off.
- Each time your head separates, it snaps back.
- Delight spiral by going farther and farther away and with crazier facial expressions.

SUPERPOWERS / CONTROLLING

LOUDMOUTH

When will he ever stop talking?

LIE ON THE FLOOR WITH THE KIDS AROUND YOU

OPEN TRANSDUCERS CAN CAUSE RANDOM IRREGULAR PHANTOM FADING IN THE MP3 WAVEFORM. EXPERT ANALYSIS AFFIRMS IT IS OPTIMAL TO MIX DOWN USING A CLEAN 48K FREQUENCY AND EQ USING A DAW PREAMP...

RAMBLE CONTINUOUSLY WITH LOTS OF JARGON.

THE KIDS TRY TO STOP YOU WITH THEIR HANDS. YOU CAN MOVE YOUR HEAD IF NEEDED BUT NOT YOUR BODY.

BUT, MAGICALLY, EACH POKE/PUSH/PULL/SQUEEZE...

SQUEAK OF A SQUEAKER, MCSQUEAK OF THE SQUEAKY LA SQUEAK SQUAWK...

CAN CHANGE YOUR VOICE...

THE SECOND DERIVATIVE EFFECTIVELY COMPUTES THAT E TO THE I PI EQUALS NEGATIVE ONE.

OR THE TOPIC...

BLOOP!

OR BE A BUTTON FOR SOUND EFFECTS.

ANTICIPATION:	Get in position and start talking rapidly	
ENLIVENING:	Exaggerate talking through all the mouth mistreatment	
TENSITY:	How often you move your head away	
UNCERTAINTY:	What you say, voice adjustment, mix in funny sounds	
FLUIDITY:	Move your head to get out of total containment	

FUN	
TIME	
COMPLEXITY	
DANGER	
KID EFFORT	
EXERTION	

MIN AGE:	Toddler
MAX AGE:	School Age
LOCATION:	Any
MATERIALS:	-
PLAYERS:	1 -3 kids

Description

- The fun in this game is fueled by the effect that, while they are trying to stop you from talking, they are causing funny changes to occur each time they touch you.
- I sometimes play this like I'm a radio, and each time they poke, I change stations to a new random one.
- Be forewarned: someone is almost certainly going to poke you in the eye to see what happens.

	Kid	Adult
Expectation	Stop Daddy from talking	Kids will mess with your face
Challenge	Daddy's head moves	Talking continuously about random things in your radio announcer voice
Fulfillment	Smooshing Daddy's face and hearing funny sounds	Exercising your improv talking skills

Example Sounds

- Poking throat makes gurgle sound
- Fingers in ears makes monotone robot voice
- Pulling on eyebrows makes deep bass voice
- Smashing nose makes police siren sound
- Fingers up nose brings out the mad man voice
- Squeezing lips makes flatulence sound

Group Adaptation

This is a great one for groups of 2 or 3.

Age

You can try this with infants, but it generally falls under the category of them just liking to bop your nose.

Variation

Face Sounds ▪ ▪ ▪ ▪ ▪ ▬

- You make noises and they try to stop you by covering your mouth
- If cover for too long, you puff out cheeks and they need to pop them
- When they do, make a long balloon-popping sound and motion, blowing them away.

Similar to

- Monster Button
- Body Noises

WALK ON THE CEILING
One small step for kid-kind

- In a room with a low enough ceiling, lift your kid upside-down, holding onto his hips.
- Have the kid walk around on the ceiling as you try to anticipate (or direct) where he wants to go.
- Obviously, it is important that your kid is small enough and you are tall and strong enough to safely do this.

SUPERPOWERS / FLYING

FUN	
TIME	
COMPLEXITY	
DANGER	
KID EFFORT	
EXERTION	

MIN AGE: Infant
MAX AGE: Preschooler
LOCATION: Room with low ceiling
MATERIALS: -
PLAYERS: 1 kid

TRAMPOLINE WATERBALLOONS
Wet bouncing balls of wetness

- Do this in a trampoline with a net cage using waterballoons that you fill up 30 at a time.
- Basically, you turn your kids loose with 100 small waterballoons in the trampoline. As they bounce around, the waterballoons go flying and everything gets wet.
- They get to kick and punch and toss them around, making a total mess that is easier to clean up than in the yard.

SUPERPOWERS / DESTROYING

FUN	
TIME	
COMPLEXITY	
DANGER	
KID EFFORT	
EXERTION	

MIN AGE: Toddler
MAX AGE: -
LOCATION: Trampoline
MATERIALS: Waterballoons
PLAYERS: 1-5 kids

ICEBERG
Floating on a book ice self

- For kids that can sit or crawl, sit them on a large board book on a carpeted floor and slide them around.
- You can have them crash into other books or try to get them to transfer onto them.

SUPERPOWERS / FLYING / FLOATING

FUN	
TIME	
COMPLEXITY	
DANGER	
KID EFFORT	
EXERTION	

MIN AGE: Infant
MAX AGE: Infant
LOCATION: Carpet
MATERIALS: Board book
PLAYERS: 1 kid

FUN	▓▓▓▓▓▓░░
TIME	▓░░░░░░░
COMPLEXITY	▓▓▓▓░░░░
DANGER	▓▓▓▓▓░░░
KID EFFORT	▓▓▓▓▓░░░
EXERTION	▓▓▓▓▓▓░░

MIN AGE: Infant
MAX AGE: Toddler
LOCATION: Any
MATERIALS: -
PLAYERS: 1 kid

LEVITATE
Standing in mid-air

- Hold the kid's feet while she is scrunched up in a ball in your arms. She should be facing away from you, leaning her back against your chest.
- Slowly have her stand up, letting her lean back against you as needed.
- When she feels comfortable, move her out away from your body so she is standing on your hands out in front of you.

SUPERPOWERS / FLYING / FLOATING

FUN	▓▓▓▓▓▓░░
TIME	▓▓░░░░░░
COMPLEXITY	▓▓▓░░░░░
DANGER	▓▓▓░░░░░
KID EFFORT	▓▓▓▓░░░░
EXERTION	▓▓▓▓▓▓░░

MIN AGE: -
MAX AGE: Preschooler
LOCATION: Any
MATERIALS: -
PLAYERS: 1 kid

LET'S JET
Fly through the wild blue yonder

- Lift your kid up and have her wrap her legs around your chest or waist, facing down
- Have her extend her arms out like wings.
- Say, "Pilot, are you ready?" and on the affirmative say, "Then let's jet!"
- Run around making flying noises.
- You can add game elements of shooting, steering, turbo speed, and more.
- We usual end by me throwing her on her bed.

SUPERPOWERS / FLYING

FUN	▓▓▓▓▓▓░░
TIME	▓▓░░░░░░
COMPLEXITY	▓▓▓░░░░░
DANGER	▓▓▓▓░░░░
KID EFFORT	▓▓▓▓░░░░
EXERTION	▓▓▓▓░░░░

MIN AGE: Infant
MAX AGE: Toddler
LOCATION: Any
MATERIALS: -
PLAYERS: 1 kid

SUPER RUNS
Faster than a speeding toddler

- Hold hands while she stands in front of you, facing the same direction.
- After a RSG, assist her in running faster than she can actually run.
- This is especially fun for toddlers who are just learning to walk and an not yet able to run on their own yet.

SUPERPOWERS / RUNNING

DELIGHTS

BEING FOUND
- Peek-a-Boo
- Covert Covers

CUDDLING
- Cuddle

BEING COVERED
- Ready Layer 1

ROLLING
- Rolling Down Hills
- Log Rolling
- Pillow Plane Coming in for a Landing

BEING SMASHED
- Swamp Creature
- Kiss Bombs

BEING KISSED
- Quirky Kisses
- Not Enough Kisses

BEING TICKLED
- Acid Rain
- Ticklefish
- Countdown

SWINGING
- Rowboat
- Hammock Swing
- Zip Swing
- Handlebar Swing

BEING SMASHED
- Crush Me
- Sandwich
- Sitdown Game
- Drop the Hammer

FLIPPING
- Catapult
- Flips
- Loops
- Flipperoo
- Flipper

FALLING
- Trust Falls
- Ejector Seat
- Blast Off Slide Down
- Space Trash

SLIDING
- Hammock Slide
- Legslide
- Home

BEING CELEBRATED
- Face Sounds

BEING SURPRISED
- Snot Sneeze
- Fire Hydrant
- Morning Surprises

CHAPTER 5
Delights

Simple amusements with the focus of giving the child temporary elation.

SWAMP CREATURE

Beware the vomit of the swamp creature!

THEY AWAKENED IT WITH THE BEATING OF THE DRUMS!

BEWARE! THE VOMIT OF THE SWAMP CREATURE!

BLAHRG!

104

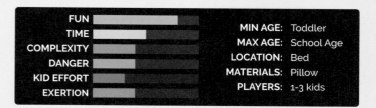

FUN	
TIME	
COMPLEXITY	
DANGER	
KID EFFORT	
EXERTION	

MIN AGE: Toddler
MAX AGE: School Age
LOCATION: Bed
MATERIALS: Pillow
PLAYERS: 1-3 kids

Description

- Turn off lights, set the kid in bed, and turn on a heartbeat sound machine to max volume.
- Tell an intro story, something to the effect of:

> *"In the middle of the ocean there is a forgotten island where once a year, on this very night, the villagers awaken a hideous swamp creature with the beating of their drums. The swamp creature slowly crawls out of its fowl pit, emerging on to the moonlit beach. But as it breaths in its first breath of the warm sea air, the sweet fragrance of flowers and trees make its stomach turn until it is certain it will retch. Beware the vomit of the swamp creature!"*

- Make lots of gross hacking noises, and then "vomit" by chucking a huge stuffed ball or pillow across the room into the bed/crib.
- For younger kids, I loft the vomit, but for older kids I throw it right at their faces.
- Go over and grab the vomit, then head back across the room to repeat the process, skipping the intro story.

Commentary

As you iterate, use colorful variations of diction to keep it interesting, such as:
- projectile vomit
- disgorgement
- foul wretchedness
- nauseated spew
- vile regurgitation

Sitdown Game
Something's lumpy in this chair

DELIGHTS / BEING SMUSHED

I THINK I AM GOING TO SIT DOWN NOW...

OH, THIS CHAIR IS LUMPY!

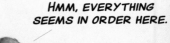

HMM, EVERYTHING SEEMS IN ORDER HERE.

Description

- In front of a sofa chair (with plenty of cushion), announce, "I think I'm going to sit in the chair."
- The kid runs behind you and jumps in underneath you. You pretend not to see this, gently sitting down on top of her.
- Do a lot of wiggling and make comments like, "Oh this chair is lumpy."
- Stand up and inspect the chair cushions in a way that the kid can escape behind you without being seen.
- Say, "Hmm, everything seems to be in order here." As you turn around, the kid jumps back in and you sit on top of her again. Repeat.
- This one is more about acting than anything else. Make sure to mix up the directions you turn and how fast you turn around.
- You need to gently "smush" the kid, but only very briefly and never to a point of the game losing its fun for her.
- She can also hold onto your belt as you swing around, and you can try surprise her by sitting on the arm of the chair, the floor, etc.

ANTICIPATION:	"I think I'm going to sit in the chair"	FUN	
ENLIVENING:	Commentary, acting like you don't see her	TIME	
TENSITY:	Duration of acting, how hard you sit on her	COMPLEXITY	
UNCERTAINTY:	When will he see me?	DANGER	
FLUIDITY:	Repeat several times. After you finally catch her, you can transition to Space Trash or Flips.	KID EFFORT	
		EXERTION	

MIN AGE: Toddler
MAX AGE: School Age
LOCATION: -
MATERIALS: Couch
PLAYERS: 1 kid

Sandwich

Assemble a couch-cushion-lunch out of them

DELIGHTS / BEING SMUSHED

MMM, I FEEL LIKE A LESLIE SANDWICH.

SOMEHOW, TRY TO EAT THE WHOLE SANDWICH.

Description

- While sitting by two large couch cushions say, "Mmm, I feel like a [child's name] sandwich."
- Pretend that the cushions are bread slices and work together to put on imaginary toppings.
- Eventually put her in the sandwich as the main ingredient.
- Put the other cushion on top, pick up the whole sandwich, and try to eat it.
- In trying to eat it, she somehow slips out.
- Start over

Example Ingredient Actions

- Set on sandwich (e.g. lettuce, tomato, cheese, pepperoni)
- Squirt on sandwich (e.g. ketchup, mustard, BBQ sauce)
- Sprinkle on sandwich (e.g. salt, pepper, popcorn)
- Pour on sandwich (e.g. hot sauce, chocolate syrup)
- Spread on sandwich (e.g. mayo, jam, peanut butter)
- Silly stuff (e.g. ice cream)

	Kid	Adult
Expectation	Make a sandwich	Make a sandwich
Challenge	Applying lots of ingredients	Thinking up funny ingredients
Fulfillment	Getting eaten	How am I going to eat this?

ANTICIPATION:	"Mmm, I feel like a [child's name] sandwich"	
ENLIVENING:	Active pretending in suggesting/applying ingredients	
TENSITY:	Ease of escape, number of ingredients	
UNCERTAINTY:	Getting away, adding silly ingredients (e.g. ice cream)	
FLUIDITY:	End with a cuddle hug	

FUN
TIME
COMPLEXITY
DANGER
KID EFFORT
EXERTION

MIN AGE: Infant
MAX AGE: Preschooler
LOCATION: Carpet
MATERIALS: Couch cushions
PLAYERS: 1 kid

BLAST OFF / SLIDE DOWN

What gets flung up, must slide down

DELIGHTS / FALLING

3... 2... 1...

HOLD HER IN YOUR PALM AND LAUNCH HER.

BLAST OFF!

THEN HAVE HER SLIDE DOWN YOUR LEGS.

Description

- While lying on your back, put your legs up on the arm of a couch.
- Have the kid sit in the palm of hand and do a countdown. On "Blast Off!" throw her onto the couch.
- She then goes over to your feet and slides or rolls down your legs.
- If you are able, it is fun to launch the kid up high enough that she can land on her feet on the couch.
- When sliding down, it helps to hold onto kid's foot so she doesn't fall off to the side.
- This game only works for kids light enough for you to launch. If they are too heavy, it is painful for you and boring for them.

Variation

EJECTOR SEAT ■.■.■.■

- Start with the same setup, but before launch, you ask questions, like "Spell DAD".
- Depending on the kid, either getting it right or wrong sends her into the couch:
  - If she wants it, then she needs to be right to get ejected.
  - If she is apprehensive, then getting it wrong can send her flying.

ANTICIPATION:	"T minus 3... 2... 1..."	
ENLIVENING:	Robot voice, Continuous stream of machine noises	
TENSITY:	Speed of operation, how wild the movements are	
UNCERTAINTY:	What will the next move be?	
FLUIDITY:	End in a hug, and you can either start again or transition to similar games like Chestboard or Flipper	

FUN

TIME

COMPLEXITY

DANGER

KID EFFORT

EXERTION

MIN AGE: Toddler
MAX AGE: Preschooler
LOCATION: Carpet
MATERIALS: Couch
PLAYERS: 1 kid

SPACE TRASH

Drop your kid into couch space

SPACE TRASH!

Description

- Start by picking up your kid and holding her horizontally over a cushiony couch. Hold her with your arms curled around her so that she can unravel.
- After a "Ready, set, go," say: "SPACE TRASH!"
- Then unravel your arms in a jerky motion and drop her spinning on the couch.
- I try to make sure she gets a full rotation in the air so that she lands on her backside.
- This game is a reference to the scene in Spaceballs where they drop off the trash in space. That scene has nothing to do with falling, or kids, but hey, that is where it got its name.

ANTICIPATION:	"SPACE TRASH"
ENLIVENING:	SFX, successive stages of "clunking" as she goes down
TENSITY:	Height of dropping, amount of spin
UNCERTAINTY:	Timing, spinning
FLUIDITY:	I usually pick them up and do it again several times.

FUN
TIME
COMPLEXITY
DANGER
KID EFFORT
EXERTION

MIN AGE:	Toddler
MAX AGE:	Preschooler
LOCATION:	Couch
MATERIALS:	-
PLAYERS:	1 kid

Flipper

Flip your kid around into a hug position

DELIGHTS / FLIPPING

READY...

SET...

Description

- This is a classic go-to for us, as the kids often find me lying on the ground and they instinctively jump aboard.
- The child should hold onto your legs at the knee, but she needs to let go at the appointed time or else nothing happens.
- Make sure to hold the child's hips so she can rotate around them. Pretty much any other axis of rotation will not work.
- I often end in a sitting position, rather than on my back, with her landing out in front of me.

Age

Kids age out of this once they are too tall to be able to rotate around. It is a sad day when you realize that.

NOW HOLD ONTO HER HIPS

GO!

110

ANTICIPATION: RSG
ENLIVENING: Crescendo, jiggle legs before start like a rocket launch
TENSITY: Speed, How closely you hold the child
UNCERTAINTY: Uneven launch timing and pacing, lateral leg movement
FLUIDITY: Transitions well into Chestboard and log rolling

FUN		
TIME		
COMPLEXITY		
DANGER		
KID EFFORT		
EXERTION		

MIN AGE: Infant
MAX AGE: Preschooler
LOCATION: Carpet
MATERIALS: -
PLAYERS: 1 kid

VARIATIONS

LOOPS ■ _ ■ _ ■ ■

- Sit in a chair with your kid's back on your thighs, his head by your knees.
- While holding his shoulders, have him bring his knees up to his chest.
- Spread your knees apart slightly so there is room for his head to pass through as he flips around into a standing position.
- Lift him slightly so that he lands on his feet. Then repeat.

FLIPPEROO ■ _ ■ ■ ■

- While you lie on your back, the kid lies face down on your shins, shoulders at your knees.
- Raise your legs up and flip her around so she lands just beyond your head.
- You can try to have her land on her feet, but generally I roll backwards and have her land on her bottom.

CATAPULT ■ _ ■ ■ _ ■

- Lie down near a couch or a low bed with your legs bent and have your kid lie on your shins, facing you.
- While holding onto his shoulders, quickly swing your feet up toward the couch, sending him upside down and landing on his back on the couch.
- You can have a story-based purpose (e.g. trebuchet for attacking the couch clan) and random launch time (e.g. breaking of a rope).
- Some kids might not like this sensation, and it is a risky maneuver—be careful.

DROP ⚒ HAMMER

Countdown to crushing time

- This is a simple bedtime antic we would do, where you are lying beside the kid in bed and out of nowhere you raise up your elbow and say: "3...2...1...DROP THE HAMMER!"
- On "DROP THE HAMMER" you bring your elbow down into the kid's abdomen with lots of embellishment (e.g. vicarious commentary, sawing/digging motions, etc.).

DELIGHTS / BEING SMUSHED

3...2...1... DROP THE HAMMER!

FUN	▰▰▰
TIME	▰
COMPLEXITY	▰
DANGER	▰▰
KID EFFORT	▰
EXERTION	▰▰▰

MIN AGE: Preschooler
MAX AGE: School Age
LOCATION: Bed
MATERIALS: -
PLAYERS: 1 kid

COUNTDOWN

Tickles are ever only seconds away

- Sit with the kid sitting in your lap, facing out, your arms around her.
- Ask for a language and a number.
  - e.g. Spanish and 5
- Count down in that language
- At 0, wait an extra second to build anticipation and then do an explosive tickle with explosion sounds.
- If you don't know the language, make it up.

DELIGHTS / BEING TICKLED

FUN	▰▰▰
TIME	▰▰
COMPLEXITY	▰▰
DANGER	▰
KID EFFORT	▰▰
EXERTION	▰

MIN AGE: Toddler
MAX AGE: Preschooler
LOCATION: Any
MATERIALS: -
PLAYERS: 1 kid

SNOT SNEEZE

Whoa, where did that come from?

- Snot Sneeze is just pretending to sneeze on your kid, but, "surprisingly," a random object comes flying at him each time.
- Any type of object that can fit in your hand will do.
- Try to conceal the object as you bring your hands up to your mouth and nose.
- Then toss it out at him while making a sneezing noise.

DELIGHTS / BEING SURPRISED

FUN	▰▰▰
TIME	▰
COMPLEXITY	▰▰
DANGER	▰
KID EFFORT	▰
EXERTION	▰

MIN AGE: Infant
MAX AGE: School Age
LOCATION: Any
MATERIALS: Something to sneeze
PLAYERS: 1-2 kids

Kiss Bombs
So much emotion in a little package

- You blow kisses from a distance that fly slowly through the air, but they are little bombs that explode as tickles when they land on the kid.
- Initially, you walk the kiss over to her after you blow it so that she learns the premise of kiss bombs.
- Later on, you can just throw them across the room, and she will play along by acting out the explosion on herself.
- When she throws a kiss back, make sure that it nearly knocks you down. Tell her she is a good kisser.

DELIGHTS / BEING KISSED

QUIRKY KISSES
Love makes people do strange things

Kiss your fingers like you are going to blow a kiss, but instead of blowing the kiss, you move your hand towards her lips as though you are going to press the kiss onto her lips, but instead of doing that, do something unexpected like:
- poke it on her forehead, or
- wipe it across her face, or
- rub it up her nose, or
- have it get stuck in her hair, or...

DELIGHTS / BEING KISSED

FUN	▓▓▓▓▓
TIME	▓
COMPLEXITY	▓
DANGER	▓
KID EFFORT	▓▓
EXERTION	▓▓

MIN AGE: Toddler
MAX AGE: School Age
LOCATION: Any
MATERIALS: -
PLAYERS: 1 kid

Not Enough Kisses
Let it never be said about me!

- At bedtime, give your kid a kiss goodnight.
- Then she says, "Not enough kisses."
- You say in a sterotypical French accent: "Let it never be said about me!" and smother her with more kisses.
- This usually repeats several times.

DELIGHTS / BEING KISSED

FUN	▓▓▓▓▓
TIME	▓
COMPLEXITY	▓▓
DANGER	▓▓
KID EFFORT	▓▓
EXERTION	▓▓

MIN AGE: Toddler
MAX AGE: Preschooler
LOCATION: Bed
MATERIALS: Pillow
PLAYERS: 1-2 kids

CONTROL TOWER, COME IN. DO YOU COPY?

PILLOW PLANE COMING IN FOR A LANDING
and her bed is the runway

- With the child standing in her bed, take her pillow and go over to the door.
- In a muffled walkie-talkie voice say something like, "Control tower, this is flight W344 on my approach, am I clear for a landing?"
- She replies in her walkie-talkie voice.
- Either way I say "Roger that, pillow plane coming in for a landing", make loud airplane engine noises, and launch the pillow at her.

DELIGHTS / BEING SMASHED

Legslide

Except for kneecaps, your legs make a good slide

DELIGHTS / FALLING / SLIDING

READY...
SET...
GO!

SIT ON THE EDGE OF A CHAIR WITH YOUR LEGS STRAIGHT OUT, SEPARATED A BIT.

LET HIM SLIDE DOWN TO YOUR FEET. REPEAT.

Description

- The chair cannot be too tall or short. I found a piano bench was just right for us.
- The child's bottom goes between your legs, with his legs spread out and around, bent at the knees.
- You can control the speed by slightly changing how close or separated your legs are.

Group Adaptation

One child can go at a time, so they need to take turns if there is a group.

Variation

You can log roll the child down your legs.

Similar to **Blast Off / Slide Down**

ANTICIPATION: RSG	
ENLIVENING: SFX (swoosh sound)	
TENSITY: Speed/Spacing between legs	
UNCERTAINTY: Will it go smoothly this time?	
FLUIDITY: This is easily and rapidly repeatable.	

FUN
TIME
COMPLEXITY
DANGER
KID EFFORT
EXERTION

MIN AGE: Toddler
MAX AGE: Preschooler
LOCATION: Any
MATERIALS: Chair
PLAYERS: 1-3 kids

ROWBOAT

Rocking and rowing on your back

READY... SET... GO!

ROW, ROW, ROW YOUR BOAT...

Description

- Lie on your back with your knees up and legs bent.
- Put the baby on your bottom with his head resting on your feet
- Then hold the baby's hands as you rock back and forth singing "Row Your Boat"
- My youngest did well at this starting around 4 months old.
- As the kid gets older, this one becomes increasingly like that Viking ship carnival ride, with big rocking motions.

Levels

- You hold baby's hands
- Baby holds onto your legs
- Wild rocking

Group Adaptation

This one is not well suited for groups, as the turns are quite long and take time to get set up correctly.

ANTICIPATION:	RSG
ENLIVENING:	Singing "Row, Row, Row Your Boat"
TENSITY:	Height of rocking motion, speed, how tightly you hold him
UNCERTAINTY:	Height of rocking
FLUIDITY:	You can do this a couple of times before transitioning to another activity

FUN	
TIME	
COMPLEXITY	
DANGER	
KID EFFORT	
EXERTION	

MIN AGE:	Infant
MAX AGE:	Toddler
LOCATION:	Carpet
MATERIALS:	-
PLAYERS:	1 kid

Morning Surprises

Start every morning with something special

SHOOT BY ROLLING
THE BALL DOWN
THE BANISTER

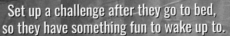

Set up a challenge after they go to bed,
so they have something fun to wake up to.

HOMEMADE SABER SWORD

Home

Celebrate their coming home, like a parade for them everyday

WHITNEY'S HOME!

WHITNEY, ARE YOU HOME?

WHITNEY'S HOME!

NUGA-NUGA-NUGA. WELCOME HOME WHITNEY. I LOVE YOU.

Description

- The idea behind this is that I always wanted my kids to be happy when they think of home. So when they get home from school, I almost make a parade out it. It is a way of celebrating them each day.
- I generally put her on my shoulder, starting a slow but accelerating marching chant that culminates in getting tossed on the couch for a tickle-kiss.
- Sometimes I switch up what we do. For example, sometimes we chase, sometimes she sits on my shoulders, sometimes she is on my back.

- I have a different version for each child. For example, Dylan's involves a chase, capture, spinning, kiss on couch with an "I love you Dylan. Welcome home."
- These can get more elaborate with age, involving surprises and randomizing what will happen.
- Generally, this is a once per day activity (hence, not rapidly repeatable).

ANTICIPATION:	"[Name], are you home?"	FUN	
ENLIVENING:	Chanting, bouncing as you go, accelerating	TIME	
TENSITY:	Speed, duration of spin	COMPLEXITY	
UNCERTAINTY:	Mixing up what will happen	DANGER	
FLUIDITY:	Easily transitions to other games like DodgeArm	KID EFFORT	
		EXERTION	

MIN AGE:	Infant
MAX AGE:	School Age
LOCATION:	Home
MATERIALS:	-
PLAYERS:	1 kid

PART 2

THE PLAY EXPERIENCE

CHAPTER 6

Roles and Responsibilities

The Child's Role: Explore play courageously

The child's role in play is quite simple: to explore play courageously. While there must still be boundaries for what is safe and good, children should have the freedom to lean into the merrymaking without fear of ridicule or physical harm. They should be encouraged to step into the action even when they do not have complete understanding of the rules or of what will happen, or to step into the story even when the rendering in their own mind is still forming.

The key ingredient for this to work is for them to trust you, which in turn depends a lot on how well you demonstrate you can carry out your role in play (for you are always playing a role in your child's play, whether you intend to or not).

Your Role: Love your kids playfully

Don't be a Gamemaster

Let's pretend you decide to start a new career. Your new job is to play with your kids. That doesn't sound so bad, right? Well in this case, you only get paid when they are delighted by play, and there is constant competition working against you (mostly in the form of electronic devices).

It has the promise of being a very fulfilling job, and you want to do your best, so you set out to be the Gamemaster. But even if it is your nature to be playful, and even if you work diligently, beware: in your efforts to be the Gamemaster, you will likely become something else entirely, something counterproductive to your goal.

"You play by my rules or I'll have another child who will."

Game Bully

Demands his own way

Thinks he is the Gamemaster by taking command. He is inflexible and unaware of the kid's level of enjoyment. He is certain that he knows the best way to play the game and how to have the most fun (if only the kids would cooperate).

Outcome: Demoralized kids

Advice: Your kids want to play with you, not for you.

"I am the greatest!"

Game Conqueror

In it for his own fun and glory

Thinks he is the Gamemaster by being the champion. He is overly competitive and sometimes physically reckless, forgetting he is playing with humans half his size. He might even let the kids take the lead, so long as he wins in the end ("I mean come on, I can't let them tell others they beat their dad").

Outcome: Discouraged kids

Advice: U before I, except in "I don't want to play with you."

"...and as stated in paragraph 3 of subsection 149.23b..."

Game Lawyer

Too many rules

Thinks he is the Gamemaster by being the ultimate referee and legislator. He is so wrapped up in all the rules necessary for supreme fairness that the game can hardly begin.

Outcome: Bored kids

Advice: Listen more than you play, play more than you speak.

"I don't know. What do you want to do?"

Game Wimp

Passively passive

He avoids taking charge, so it doesn't even occur to him to be a Gamemaster. He lacks direction, so he abdicates leadership, thinking he is "empowering" his kids. But he is willing to play (as long as they do all the work).

Outcome: Tyrant or uninspired kids, short-lived play

Advice: Be the one who takes responsibility to make things fun (it's okay to drive).

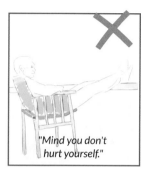

"Mind you don't hurt yourself."

Game Chaperone

Watching from a distance

Thinks he is the Gamemaster by keeping an eye on things, albeit from a distance. He is above the silliness of child's play, being primarily concerned that no one gets hurt. He closely watches the clock to let everyone know when gametime is over.

Outcome: Kids playing video games instead

Advice: Get your hands dirty.

"My show must go on."

Game Clown

Steals the spotlight

Thinks he is the Gamemaster by entertaining everyone with constant over-the-top theatrics and silliness. Sometimes the kids laugh, but he makes them stay quiet for his frequent monologues. He is great at staying in character, enough so that he forgets the kids are even there or that they want to play too.

Outcome: Kids feeling awkward, becoming inactive consumers

Advice: Don't perform for them, play with them.

Even though I know better, I still catch myself falling into these imbalance traps. I have found that if you want to be fun to play with, don't try to be a Gamemaster. Trying to master game management will leave you focusing on the rules, or winning, or orderly conduct, or safety, or even your own comfort, while neglecting the fundamental goal. So don't try to be a Gamemaster; instead, **love your kids playfully**, because if you have a great time loving your kids while you play together, you will become the Gamemaster in their eyes.

Love your kids playfully

The Hospitality of Play

A better analogy of the role to assume when playing with your kids is to be a Happy Host. When I think of a Happy Host, I think of a confident gentleman, someone who invites a friend to his home and welcomes her in with a smile, sets the agenda and the house rules as needed, controls the ambience to ensure his guest is comfortable, and ultimately is focused on serving his guest, making sure she has a great time.

Translating that to gameplay looks like this:

The Happy Host...	Likewise, I should...
Invites a guest to his home	Initiate playtime
Welcomes her in with a smile	Put on my game face and say "yes"
Sets the agenda	Stay at least one step ahead with a basic plan of what to do next
Establishes the house rules	Quickly provide the game structure
Actively facilitates the activities	Be on point to maintain momentum through transitions
Has an authentically good time with the guest	Play for mutual fun, not out of guilt
Gracefully brings the evening to a close	Know when to end, and end well
Cleans up after the guest	Take responsibility to clean up
Steadily attends to the guest's experience	Be a servant leader

Initiating playtime

Usually my kids come to me and ask to play, but it is magical to them when I come to them unexpectedly, excited to play. They jump with delight, and it begins.

Put on your game face

When it is time to play, you need to put on your game face, even if it is after a long day of work or when your energy is spent and you only want to rest. I do not mean put on your "poker face," acting emotionlessly or inauthentically as if your problems do not exist. I mean you need to defy passivity and say, "Yes," even when your logic thinks, "Not right now," so that your burdens from work and life do not steal a special moment with your kids. When it is time to play, don't bring anything into the game that does not belong (including your stress, negative attitude, or phone) so that your kids can feel how important they are to you.

Forethought of what we will play

For impromptu play, there is not much time for preparation, but you cannot go into it like the Game Wimp saying, "I don't know, what do you want to do?" Avoid this by picking at least a first step and then initiating the play. Sometimes they will come to you, begging for their favorite game. In those cases, you might choose to start with some entry games that build up to that one. This is where it helps to know how to establish a good playtime arc, as described in Chapter 11.

Frame the game and how we will play it

When you decide on a game, it is your role to set up the game quickly. The essential rules of new games should be articulated clearly up front—but only the essential ones, the ones that if you did not state them up front, you would have to completely interrupt the gameplay to explain. You can introduce clarifying rules as needed later on, but do so as a way of evolving the gameplay into something better, rather than for restarting broken gameplay. Also, if the game involves props, take it upon yourself to set them up correctly the first time.

All this is done for a quick onramp to fun. It is not so much about making things easier for your kids as it is about minimizing or even preventing the boring parts of gameplay.

Foresight of when gameplay should change

Just as you need forethought before play begins, you also need foresight during play to anticipate optimal transition points. This maintains the momentum of fun, and is discussed in more detail in Chapters 7 and 11.

Fun play should be mutual

Though I am describing play as a service to your kids, it is actually more fun for them when you are enjoying it too. If you are not having fun, they will pick up on that, but if you are having a blast, it is contagious, and they will have a blast too. At a minimum, whether you are doing it for fun or to see your kids have fun, you need to want to play the game, and it is up to you to figure out how to have a good time.

Concluding peacefully

If a game is progressing nicely but ends abruptly, your kids are going to want to continue, working against your efforts to transition out of play. It requires being a bit artful, but by knowing how to read your kids, subtly setting expectations along the way and patiently waiting for the natural transition points, you will be able to find a smooth resolution, which in my family generally involved us lying on the ground, my arm around my kid, looking up at the sky, saying, "I love you," complimenting them, and then planning the rest of the day.

Cleaning up after the guest

When our game time is over, I see it as my responsibility that things get cleaned up. I might encourage my kids to help, but I try to make that a fun invitation rather than a command (e.g. getting the blocks back into the bin by shooting hoops with them).

Be a servant leader

Being the Happy Host is a form of servant leadership where you take charge without taking over. Your kids look to you to be a leader, directing the play, the rules, and the activity transitions—all while making them feel like they are in control and the best parts were their ideas. You need to do this all while in a constant feedback loop focused on your kids so that even though the fun is mutual, the purpose is to love your kid though a great play experience together.

As an adult, when you have some free time, if your initial thought is to play hide-and-seek, then you are a playful individual indeed. But for most of us, I reckon, choosing to play is a decision to show love through quality time together, when we set aside our initial desires for rest and comfort in order to play together wholeheartedly. Both sides benefit in this. For me, play is motivation enough most of the time; love fills in the gap the rest of the time.

Becoming Better at Your Role

The Continuous Feedback Loop

The Game Conqueror, Game Lawyer, Game Wimp, and all the others have something in common: they unknowingly cared about something else more than the child, be it winning, or adhering to the rules, or their own comfort. What the Happy Host got right was focusing on loving his child. But how do you do that in a game? What does that actually look like?

I have come to see that the key principle here is to **carefully listen and then respond in creative kindness**. In gameplay, your decision of what to do next is informed primarily by situational awareness: whatever feedback you can gather in the moment regarding the game, the players, and the environment. That helps you determine if the gameplay needs something more, something less, or something different. But doing this well means going beyond mere situational awareness; you need to also incorporate principles of gameplay, your intimate knowledge of the child, and your own creative contributions before deciding how you will respond.

Interestingly enough, I believe the child is following a similar, simpler thought process at the same time as you. However, for her it is more focused on responding to what she predicts will happen, rather than determining what should happen next.

127

When done well, the feedback loop will help you propel the gameplay experience forward and maintain its momentum. When done poorly, you will pick up on cues of the child losing interest or wanting to play something else. When the feedback loop is disregarded, the fun is usually one-sided and gameplay short-lived.

The continuous feedback loop is the crucial underlying mechanism for how the Happy Host knows if he is successful. I will be frequently referring back to it throughout this book.

Protecting the Fun

Sharing control

I don't believe a child should need to think about roles and responsibilities, she should just play. But there are times you will need to step in to prevent her from "breaking the play." A good example here is not letting her become a **tyrant**: someone who oppressively controls the direction and rules of the game, like a child version of the Game Bully.

"Too much control" looks like one person imposing exactly what the other should do, disregarding that person's own ideas and contributions. Giving the child too much control will usually ruin the fun for you, as she too will get caught in the trap of becoming a Gamemaster. On the other hand, if you command too much, then it is no fun for either of you. Balancing control is part of your role.

I've been blessed with kids that are not generally tyrants in play. My default mode is co-creative play, and over time they have come to trust my sense of what will be fun, knowing that I am always open to their creative input.

Preventing broken play with multiple children

Playing with multiple children of different ages is a learning ground for compassion and for teaching the difference between challenging and demoralizing someone. It confounds me when I see one of my kids intentionally do something that breaks the play (e.g. rudely steal the ball from the youngest player). But I use that moment as an opportunity to reinforce that that is not play, and that good play is to the benefit of everyone involved.*

The best way to see when play becomes broken is to play with a toddler, because toddlers will go directly from happy to crying when play is broken, giving you instant feedback.

Over time I have explained "play" to my kids mostly by defining what play is not:[*]

× *teasing*
- If our words or actions are making others really frustrated, that is not play, that is teasing.
  - "Monkey in the middle" games

× *bullying*
- If our words or actions are making others afraid or think less of themselves, that is not play, it is bullying.
  - Name calling, making the same person be the bad guy every time

× *recklessness*
- Accidents happen, but if people are getting physically hurt and crying, that is not play, that is recklessness.
  - Emotion-based fighting; uncontrolled, dangerous decisions

× *selfishness*
- If we are intentionally leaving someone out, that is not play, that is selfishness.
  - Saying "No" to the younger sibling who wants to join, or the new kid, or the kid with disabilities

In all my years of playing games with my kids, I cannot recall having played even once a "monkey in the middle" game, where you try to make yourself feel better at someone else's expense. And whenever I see such a dynamic emerging, I immediately change the game. I don't use broken gameplay to "toughen up my kids"; instead, I aspire to instill in them the character to courageously stand up for others and honorably change the game for the good of all involved. I am seeing this now when my kids play together, where my older kids step in to adjust the game when the younger ones are getting frustrated.

KABOOM!

Even while playing carefully, small children will fall down and get hurt. For the minor mishaps I tend to say, "Kaboom!", which acknowledges the accident but encourages getting back up and going again.

Tracking turns

When there are multiple kids involved, you need to be the one to keep track of whose turn it is. It is not glamorous, but it is one of your important responsibilities. This is because kids are just not as good at this task, and their default mentality seems to be a scarcity mindset where they need to go next or else they might never get a chance to go again.

---

* In addition to this list, as a matter of safety when they play somewhere else, we have also established a rule that we always play with our clothes on.

Being reliable in this task brings peaceful progress to the gameplay. There have been so many times when I have quieted a panicking, crying child with the words, "Do you want to go next?" and thus shifted the gameplay into turn taking. And when I am taking turns while playing one-on-one with a child, I often show generosity by giving her extra turns (especially in skill-based games). Be wary of doing that if there are multiple kids, however, as it is generally better to make sure they get relatively fair amounts of focused play.

On Saying "Yes"

One evening years ago, I was at a board meeting talking with a friend, a successful leader at Apple. We were both at very stressful points in our lives, discussing somewhat superficially the busyness of life and how fast our young kids were growing up. I decided to challenge us both to a new philosophy: that whenever our kids approach us to play, that we would say "yes," even if it was at an inopportune time, even if we didn't feel like playing. While I have not lived up to that 100%, it has enhanced my thinking on the subject, and here is why.

Fun play can be brief

When my son asks me to play Monopoly or two-person Uno, I almost always say "No, but...". Those games afford neither a rapid onramp to fun nor a convenient exit. But when he just wants to play with me, I say "Yes" as often as I can, knowing that we can have a great time even in a short time. I can craft that kind of playtime to fit the time constraints, be appropriate for the surroundings, and be fun for us both.

I would estimate that over the years the average play session with my kids lasted 10 minutes. The sweet spot was half hour sessions—those were probably where the best memories were made. The longest session was a 3.5 hour game of Uno with my son (which is why I say "no" to two-person Uno). Truthfully, the vast majority were only a minute or two long, so short that I never even tracked them.

In other words, if you are strapped for time and want to play more often with your kids, play in brief sessions, but make that time really count. Quality time does not have to require more of your time. For the mathematical among us, you could say that for the frequency of play to increase (assuming available play time is fixed), duration of play will naturally decrease. It might look like this:

$$\text{Total Play Time} = (\text{Play Frequency}) \times (\text{Play Duration})$$

If this is fixed… and this increases, …then this decreases.

Obviously you need to have some boundaries (bedtime, for example), but in principle, err on the side of saying "yes" to play.

Availability communicates value

Your time is precious, so being available to your kids communicates to them that they are precious to you. Time, by its continuous yet limited nature, is a forcing function of prioritization; it illuminates what matters most to you. Based on the previous equation, I would advocate for increasing available playtime together, which gives headroom for more frequent and longer play.

$$\text{Total Play Time} = (\text{Play Frequency}) \times (\text{Play Duration})$$

If this increases… this can go up… and/or this can go up.

Time is short

You know this already, that there will come a time all too soon when your kids will no longer play these types of games with you. There will be a final "Peek-a-Boo," a day when you row the boat for the last time, a day when they are too big to be thrown into the air or to climb onto your shoulders. In many ways you will eventually be displaced by their friends or screens. I don't recommend playing on the basis of guilt, but I do think we are all prone to lose perspective, and that we would prioritize our time differently if we could see how quickly we are approaching the turn in the road ahead.

Your role is to love your kids playfully; could there be a better job? Most of this chapter has been about loving your kids, while "playfully," well that is what the next chapter is about.

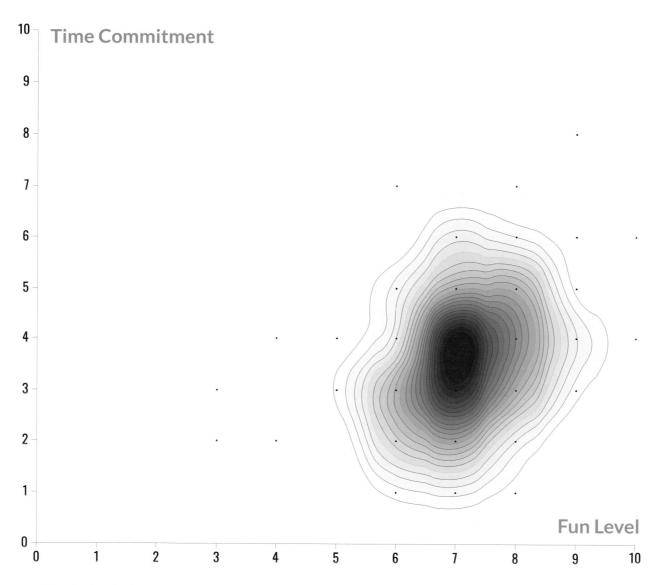

For the hundreds of different games we have played across thousands of sessions, the sweet spot has been games that are a lot of fun but not a big time commitment.

In this contour graph, each game is plotted as a black dot using my estimates of time and fun level. The density of the overlapping games is shown by the contour lines, with the darkest blue being the "sweet spot."

CHAPTER 7

Elements of the Fun

What specifically is it in the game that is fun? I have come to see it as a variety of things. My kids love the sensation of being chased, for example. In challenge games, it can be devising a strategy to attain a goal. Still in others it can be taking your best guess while you are still uncertain, or following someone into a very imaginative story. Examples like these illuminate key ingredients of gameplay that make it fun to play and result in a fulfilling outcome, such as cathartic laughter or the self-esteem of achieving a personal best.

One of the simplest forms of playing with your kids is tickling. However, tickling by itself is actually not a lot of fun. I call this **cattle prodding**, as it is an attempt at play that is momentarily stimulating, but thereafter unpleasant (and depending on the child it might be unwelcome). But tickling, when layered with the elements of fun discussed in this chapter, can become a common part of many great play experiences.*

---

* I used to joke with my wife that this book should be called "101 Ways to Tickle Your Children," since so many of the games we play involve or lead up to tickling.

Entropy and the Disengagements of Gameplay

When I want to be intentional about a great play experience with my kids, I do not rely on fun gameplay to just "happen." Even though I try to let things flow naturally, I recognize that the fun parts are the result of several factors going well with good balance and appropriate timing. When that balance breaks, the child ends up withdrawing or disconnecting from play. If left to its own devices, gameplay will always eventually diminish. I think of it like **entropy**, as though you are constantly working against the forces of decline and failure.

Entropy: gameplay, by itself, will always eventually diminish

Gameplay entropy is not evil, it is just a reality. **The goal is not for gameplay to last forever but for the child to be fulfilled when playtime ends.** You can use the fact of entropy as a basis for making the time together effective and efficient.

Entropy exists because, apart from your involvement, a young child's interest level in a game has a half-life measured in seconds*. This means that every certain number of seconds the child will lose half of the interest he previously had. To maintain interest requires your ongoing, intentional, interest-renewing adjustments, which are informed by the continuous feedback loop.

Entropy leads to kids disengaging from a game, and I have seen four types of gameplay disengagements to work against.

---

* I have not measured this precisely, but it is based on years of observation.

134

✕ Disparities

Disparities occur when there is a disappointing mismatch in expectations between you and your child. From the child's perspective, it is a quick letdown from what she thought would happen to what actually occurred. Examples include an unwelcome touch, a poorly played turn, confusion from misunderstood rules, or a sudden drop of energy or interest. Disparities are usually sudden and cause the child to briefly reassess if it is worth continuing to play. Ultimately, disparities are the cause of all the other types of gameplay disengagements. The continuous feedback loop is the best defense against disparities.

✕ Boredom

No matter how awesome the game is, there is always something in the back of the kid's mind hoping that the next round will be even better. I believe that in gameplay, boredom is the result of a mental fatigue in hoping for an improvement that just does not come, leaving the child disappointed with what is already in hand. No game is immune to boredom, as even the best games will lose their magic unless you intervene to create renewed interest. Boredom surfaces gradually, can arise from stagnant or unchallenging gameplay, and is preventable through mutual engagement (and inevitable without it).

✕ Exhaustion

Exhaustion is the physical twin of boredom, for just as the mind will tire from overly repetitive gameplay, the body will eventually become exhausted from continuous exertion in gameplay. There will always be an end to gameplay, but it does not have to end with exhaustion. Exhaustion can be avoided through well-timed transitions that enable interludes of rest and redirected interest.

✕ Discouragement

Kids become discouraged in gameplay when they are emotionally convinced they are doomed to fail, losing hope of meaningful participation and fun. When discouraged, a child resigns from gameplay or acts out in her frustration. This can easily happen when you are playing the wrong role, like when the Game Bully crushes the child's playful spirit, or when the Game Conqueror prevents the child from winning. Discouragement is avoidable by attentively adjusting to the continuous feedback loop.

Essential Ingredients of Fun Gameplay

After analyzing the games I've created with my kids over the years, I've identified several key elements that bring the fun and hold off the disengagements of gameplay. I consider these to be the essential ingredients of fun gameplay.

The Anticipation

The primary purpose of the anticipation is to build up excitement. Without it, gameplay that was intended to be fun can be dull or confusing. Going back to our tickling example, anticipation can take the form of letting the child first see you put your hands up and wiggle your fingers before going in for the tickle. This communicates a playful intention that sets the context of what's to come. It allows the child the opportunity to proactively respond, such as by trying to escape, and thus co-create a fun chase situation. Without that anticipation, you are cattle prodding, which is unexpected and generally unwelcome.

The Anticipation: communicating that something remarkable is about to happen

Using your best tool: *Ready... Set... Go!*

Exact Wording

I prefer "Ready...Set...Go" over "On your marks...get set...go", since it is simpler to say (fewer syllables) and does not imply a race. I also prefer it over "1...2...3" since we all seem to come to different conclusions as to whether we go on "3" or after it.

Protocol

The person who has the first move in the game should wait on the other person to say "Go." So while I always initiate with "Ready...Set...," I let the child say "Go" when I have the first move and need to know she is ready (e.g. Shinobi). If she has the first move (e.g. Cliffhanger), then I say the "Ready...Set..." and the "Go." I like to give her some creative control for when we begin, though that can be abused if she chooses to false start. In that case, I usually embrace it as part of her creative expression without letting it become a pattern.

Variations in Rhythm

It is important you establish a default timing for how you say this. Consistency ingrains in them a default expectation, which they will use to predict what is about to happen. However, you can adjust the timing of each part of the phrase for dynamic effect, especially if you say "Go."

R---S---G-   Default

R-----S---G-   Extending Ready is useful for providing more time for the child to get ready, such as getting into position.

R---S-----G-   Extending Set is useful for intensifying the anticipation.

RS-----G-   Shortening Ready has a similar effect as extending Set, but also implies less time is available (i.e. a faster tempo).

R---SG-   Shortening set is used to begin abruptly, usually before the child is ready.

RSG   Rapid fire RSG is used to catch the child off-guard. Use if very sparingly.

R---S---g-g-G   Trick starts should also be used sparingly as they quickly become annoying when overused. When you say something like, "Ready...Set...Monkey," you are basically playing a pre-game game (not all that fun in our experience, though they do like random object humor).

The vast majority of games I play with my kids begin with "Ready...Set...Go!" It is my most useful tool, which I have used thousands and thousands of times over the years. When you use those words to start an activity, you are *communicating that something remarkable is about to happen*, so the kids need to be prepared or they will miss it. I've used it with each of my kids since they were infants, and by 6-12 months of age, even before they could talk, they knew exactly what it meant. I would say "Ready...Set..." and by this point my one year old would tense up with excitement and smile uncontrollably.

I do not use "Ready...Set...Go!" for all games, though. Anticipations come in lots of forms, tailored to the gameplay. Some games, like Superman and Crown of Splendor, benefit by having a **pre-game anticipation**, which excites the kids into action (e.g. "It's a bird, it's a plane, it's..."). Pre-game anticipations announce the transition into a game, and they generally are used only once because they are either too monotonous or non-sequitur to use again after the game has begun. In rapidly repeatable games like Ooga Booga and Cage that Animal, **pre-play anticipations** initiate (or conclude) the play iteration and can take the form of a recognizable phrase that is specific to that game. Still, in other games, the anticipation takes the form of a countdown, because that plays into the imagined scenario (e.g. taking off in Let's Jet or the robotic nature of Bodybot).

Pre-Game Anticipations	Example
Beckoning gameplay	*Crown of Splendor*: fanfare anthem calls children to play
Falling into character	*No Fun for Anyone*: talk in mean lady voice For games like *Sleeping Giant* and *Weevil-Rat-Worm*, the mere position is enough to communicate that game play is about to begin.

Pre-Play Anticipations	Example
Enable them to be ready and excited	*Crown of Splendor*: the phrase "I am the king, this is my kingdom, and here is my throne." Swordplay: "On guard!"
Give yourself time to reset and make ready	*Rockpile*: "Get in position!" (while you position cushions)

Theoretically, every game can have an anticipation, even if it is just a momentary pause. The goal, however, is to maximize the fun by intentionally enhancing the anticipation. At a minimum, the anticipation needs to field two questions in the mind of the child:

- What's going to happen? (i.e. What's Daddy going to do?)
- What am I going to do in response?

But by enhancing the anticipation, you communicate much more information, which builds up the energy before the game begins.

who • Your body language (e.g. eye contact) can communicate it is an invitation to them

what • Aside from communicating that something remarkable is about to happen, it can provide context, such as a character role you are assuming

when • It can communicate the countdown until things begin

how / where • If needed, your body language can also communicate what they need to quickly do before things start (e.g. urgently point to get into position)

why • Perhaps most importantly, it can communicate your playful intention

Being consistent in how you use anticipations will help the child develop an understanding of how the anticipation works. This is a good thing, so don't feel like you have to be wildly creative in providing a different anticipation each time or for each game. As I've said, I predominantly use "Ready... Set... Go!" Novel, creative anticipations are useful when you introduce new games or when you are trying to use the element of surprise.

SCENARIO: You want the kids to pick up their toys before climbing into bed

UNPLAYFUL
Command them and come back in a minute (you will see they have done nothing)

PLAYFUL
Lead them on a mission by telling them that, regrettably, the earth will explode if any toys remain on its surface in 10...9... (and you jump into action to help saying, "Quick, we can make it! We can save the world!")

The Enlivening

While the anticipation communicates "Let's do this!", the **enlivening** communicates "We're really doing this!" Enlivening uses theatrics and sound effects to bring the game to life, just as an actor brings the inanimate script to life and a musician brings the inanimate score to life.

Enlivening uses theatrics and sound effects to bring the game to life

Enlivening will come naturally to some people more than others. But, being an introverted person myself who has never taken a drama class, I believe it is attainable by anyone who genuinely tries it in the audience of their kids. If you want to love your kids playfully, **you'll need to be willing to look silly.** So be silly and proud of it. Perhaps others will think you are ridiculous, but they will have no doubt you love your kids.

In my experience, I primarily enliven games in three ways:
- entering sudden reality
- stimulating multiple senses
- manipulating interest

Entering Sudden Reality

Enlivening the game to feel convincingly more real makes it more engaging, and it permits you and your child to let go temporarily of current reality in place of a more fun imagined one. I call this "**entering sudden reality**" because, for it to work, there is no in-between state and no delay permitted in getting there.

Sleeping Giant does not begin until you are noisily slumbering on the floor. Notice there is no preamble of rules; you take the lead and they make the decision whether to follow. If gameplay were like a full-length movie, there would be more time taken to set the stage, but impromptu games are more like movie trailers, where you are instantly dropped into a different world. Fall into character immediately so you do not waste any time or allow a disparity.

While this reality transitions in a flash, it is also fleeting and changeable. The scenario is short-lived, so do it well, enduring the minor inconveniences and discomforts. And if something about it is just not working, go ahead and adjust whatever you need so that you do not give a foothold to disengagements. For like all other actions you take, each next step should be informed by the continuous feedback loop. And by the way, the next step might be to follow your child's lead into a place you hadn't anticipated.

I sometimes use enlivening for reducing the competitive nature of a game. Falling into character makes it less about "you versus me" and more about "you versus the greater antagonism." For example, in Beware the Lightning the child is avoiding getting struck by lightning; he is not keeping score on how many times I got him or he jumped past me. Similarly, a two year old knows you can outrun him, but in Ooga Booga he is trying to outrun the silly, wild caveman who is chasing him.

Entering sudden reality also functions as your source for relevant creative material. If you are playing Spinning with your kids, what sound, out of all the sounds in the world, should you make to enliven the play? That depends on what you are trying to enact. Are they holding onto a planet spinning out of control? Are they running through the forest being chased by a badger? Are they hanging onto the edge of an airplane propeller? Picking off-target can lead to a disparity, while not picking at all can lead to boredom.

Another trap is thinking the "show" or even your skills are the point of the enlivening. That is the folly of the Game Clown. The whole point of the enlivening is to make the game more fun for both of you.

However, the enlivening is not just about acting. For example, I use smacktalk in contest games like Shoops. Admittedly though, the vast majority of the time I'm enlivening games primarily with sound effects.

Stimulating Multiple Senses

Just as educators know that they must teach their lessons using visual, auditory, and kinetic methods, you enhance gameplay by incorporating multiple senses. It draws the kids in and helps maintain momentum. Adding sound effects to a game is like the difference between watching a muted movie with subtitles versus cranking up the volume (the latter feels much more real). Showing the action is the difference between telling a funny story versus acting out the funny story as you tell it (the latter gets a lot more laughter).

Games that are primarily kinetic (e.g. Spinning), need sound effects added in, while games that are heavily auditory (e.g. Loudmouth) need the addition of humorous body movements. Almost every game needs awesome sound effects and ample body movements, and it is up to you to provide them.

Here are some of my favorite voices to portray when enlivening:

The Squire Crier

- Just as a knight would have a trusty apprentice who served him as an arms-bearer and helped protect him, sometimes your child needs someone to provide some vital hints or unseen context.
- "Look out!", "Quick, grab the sword!", "Oh no! It's the guardian toad!"

Vicarious Exclamations

- In games like Weevil-Rat-Worm, you can intensify the action by vocalizing the thoughts you would imagine saying if you were in the child's situation.
- "Oh no! Oh the agony! It's eating my flesh!"

Daunting Taunting

- Taking up the voice of the villain makes it more exciting for the child to imagine from whom or what she is running, and it creates a sense of urgency.
- "Get her! Don't let her escape!", "You'll never get away with this!", "Where did she go?!"

The Oblivious Observer

- Some games, like the Sitdown Game and Sandwich, require you to enact an almost blind character that cannot see precisely the thing he is looking for (which is usually the child).
- "This chair seems lumpy...", "I think I'll make a Leslie sandwich"

The Manipulation of Interest

A magician is skilled at misdirection, where he draws your attention to a hand that ultimately is not even holding the coin, while the coin slips away into a back pocket unnoticed. Music composers are also masters of shifting your focus. A choir singing in unison has our direct attention, but when the choir shifts to singing polyphony (numerous different simultaneous melody lines), our minds cannot easily follow and so they peacefully drift elsewhere.

Nimble management of the child's interest is an important part of each of the elements of fun, but the enlivening is where it takes its ultimate form. Just before your kid feels confident in the game element she is focused on, you shift her focus to a different stimulating element. Playing Asteroids is a great example of this. I always start with the basic asteroid, and as soon as the child reaches maximum delight in basic blocking (and the consequence of not), I vary the speed, the angles, the trajectory, and the type of attack (e.g. big and small asteroids)—not just to make it more challenging (tensity) or surprising, but to make it more "real." Once she has started to overcome these challenges, I do something that breaks the assumed rules (e.g. corkscrew asteroid, two asteroids at once). Then, before she gets too comfortable with blocking that, I introduce something that cannot be blocked (e.g. X-rays), requiring her to jump out of the way. This is an advanced concept in gameplay and a powerful tool for deepening interest.

Your child's interest has a half-life measured in seconds, so you need to continuously toss it around before it hits the ground. Manipulating interest is also a dynamic way of increasing the next key ingredient of fun: tensity.

ADVICE I GIVE MYSELF

Don't be lazy — show them you love them by playing with them the way they want to play.

Tensity

Tensity is maintaining fun by balancing how challenging an activity is. Even though I know my kids really well, I'm almost never exactly right at setting the level of challenge on a new activity. So we experiment and we adjust.

Adjusting the level of difficulty is crucial for avoiding entropy and for keeping the game fun for you. The fundamental principle of tensity is that **the outcome of the challenge needs to be achievable yet uncertain**. Any easier and it devolves to boredom, any harder, discouragement[*].

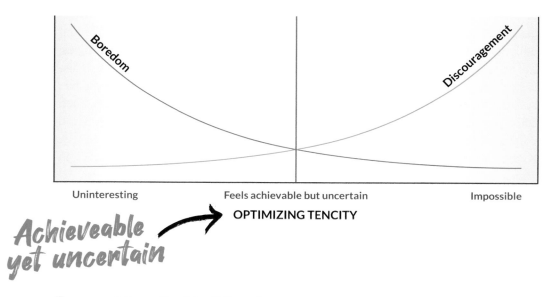

Uninteresting   Feels achievable but uncertain   Impossible

OPTIMIZING TENCITY

Achieveable yet uncertain

Types of Tensity Modifications

Incremental Difficulty

As the child's skill and understanding of the game improve, you gradually increase the difficulty, such as when you introduce new levels in Asteroids. This is the primary tensity mechanism I use. In simpler games and amusements, this can also be done by increasing the level of autonomy the child has, or in other words, decreasing the level of support you are providing the child.

---

[*] *Slightly too difficult is fine, as the child might get better with repeated attempts. But you do not want the challenge to feel impossible, or she will give up.*

Unequal Rules

You can directly optimize the rules of a skill game to balance the challenge for each player. For example, the child must make 5 shots while you must make 10 shots or 5 in a row. Another approach is to make your goal farther away or smaller (e.g. Football Shoops).

Contrived Disabilities

You can play by the same rules but have artificial limitations placed upon you to balance tensity, such as:

- not using one of your senses (e.g. Blind Monster Wrestling)
- not moving freely (e.g. you move backwards in Reverse Tag and on your knees in Juggernaut)
- not moving quickly (e.g. you move slowly in Go-Go Juice)
- not using your dominant hand (e.g. Shoops, Marble Fire)

Verbal Feedback

You can also influence tensity by providing direct feedback. For example, providing encouragement and additional instruction can help the struggling child rise to the challenge. Alternatively, "smack talk" can humble him when he is overconfident.

Fairness versus Equality

For competitive games, fairness is an important means of balancing tensity. In the games you play with your kids, rarely will "fair" be the same thing as "equal." This is because equality becomes unfair when you try to keep all the variables the same for each unique player. Instead, keep gameplay fair by adjusting variables as needed in order to balance the level of challenge.

If all players are shooting a basketball from the same spot, but you are twice the size of the others, that is in a sense equal, but unfair. Making it fair by changing where or how you shoot guarantees things will not be equal, but that's okay. Balance the tensity so that all players can win, though it is unclear who ultimately will win.

In almost all competitive games you play with your kids, you will need to stack the cards against yourself so that there is an interesting challenge for you and a hope of winning for them.

Uncertainty

When I studied to be a teacher, I learned not to ask students questions to which I already knew the answer. That form of basic knowledge test tends to turn people off and result in terse answers. Instead, you ask open-ended questions, which not only avoid one-word answers but invite the individual to distinctively express himself. In a similar way, uncertainty opens the door for more interesting possibilities. And like enlivening's manipulation of interest, it is an almost magical tool for improving the fun of a game by resetting the child's center of attention.

Randomness

Once you have established a workable game pattern, you need to change things up to maintain momentum and defy boredom. Randomness provides variety that is especially important in rapidly repeatable games, like Head Games, where each iteration should be neither identical nor predictable. It does not have to be a surprise, so it is okay for the child to know that things are changing, just not for her to be confident about what they are changing into. Keep her in a state of wonder.

Non-Linearity

Uncertainty can also be used in changing up the flow of a game, such as the timing and selection of transitions to new levels within a game or to complementary activities. What makes non-linearity uncertain for the child is that it should not be obvious which transition will happen next or even within a game how things will evolve. Yet non-linearity is not necessarily random; it is the result of paying attention to the continuous feedback loop and breaking up monotonous linearity.

Improving Your Questions

✗ "What do you want to do?" *(You should have a default plan for this already and initiate.)*

✗ "How many points do we need to make?" *(You should decide this based on tensity.)*

✓ "And then the bear turned into a...?" *(Sets context but gives some authorship—go with it.)*

I also enjoy giving my kids choice as a way of giving them authorship in the game and a sense of control. This breaks up unintentional predictability by introducing their input.

Surprise

Surprises are unexpected changes, which you can introduce in all kinds of ways during the gameplay. They prevent monotony by shifting key variables, such as the intensity of gameplay (e.g. the pace of the chase, the dynamics of the villain's voice, the timing of the start) or the mechanics of the game (e.g. intentionally breaking a rule for effect).

It is interesting that surprises work in contrast to the anticipation:

Anticipation	Surprise
Builds up expectation	Break expectation
Slower is better	Faster is better
Key ingredient in all games	Used sparingly for effect

Momentum

Momentum happens when there is smooth and satisfying transition between activities. It is an almost magical state of flow where the gameplay naturally progresses, because you and the child are connecting on the same wavelength.

The magic of momentum is that it can compensate for deficiencies in other areas (e.g. if my sound effects are unrealistic). For my youngest child, it became clear to me that as long as there's momentum, he almost didn't care which game we were playing or how well. Momentum is fun in and of itself.

Maintaining momentum requires not only being in tune with the child but the artful use of both well-timed transitions and graceful mixing.

Timing

Within a game, rapid repeatability is a strong momentum builder. That is when you iterate on the main amusement pattern with little to no restart time, such as when you send additional asteroids and when you restart Ooga Booga by using its hook phrase. I find it is fairly intuitive to time these iterations well.

Building momentum by transitioning between games is a little trickier. Ideally you anticipate the turning points in the game where something different would be better. This means you need to quickly identify a turning point, have a slightly more exciting next-game in mind, and choose the right time to enact the transition. Changing the game too early is mildly disappointing since it cuts fun play short, but waiting too long is much more detrimental (at least in active high-momentum play), as it gives entropy a solid foothold. Some detailed transition examples are in Chapter 11.

Good Mix

Some games are natural complements of each other, and so they transition nicely, such as Climb the Coconut Tree and Timber. Other games seem to work well as surprise transitions, such as Ooga Booga or DodgeArm. But for longer gameplay sessions, use a variety of delights and challenges instead of only playing similar games. For example, before getting exhausted with multiple strenuous games, switch to a mental challenge game for time to physically recover. After some skill-based games, mix in some acrobatics. Whether it is transitioning to a new level within a game or to a separate game altogether, your selection and timing are like choosing the right mix of music for the experience. Just make sure to focus on the fun more than the process.

Two Parts Confidence, One Part Crazy

I have long believed that you only need about two thirds of things figured out to move forward with a game idea*. You can embrace a new idea for your next action, being sure that it is safe, kind, and propels the gameplay forward, but being unsure of where it might lead or if it is really funny or not. Overanalyzing things and searching for perfect data slows the momentum and gives a foothold to the disengagements of play. Having just enough confidence, mixed with some silliness, builds momentum and the child's perception of your playfulness.

I am at least 67% sure of this.

CHAPTER 8

Designing Amusements

Playing with the Little Ones

You will not play with an infant in the same way as you will with a toddler or a school-aged child. The earlier stages of cognitive and physical development require a form of play that is much simpler than games.

In this area, I highly respect O. Fred Donaldson's work on Original Play*. He describes how to create an environment of safety and love by avoiding contests, grabbing, talking, and even tickling. I have found these methods to be a good starting point when first playing with infants and to some degree toddlers.

This chapter describes the mechanics of amusing children, something more fundamental than crafting the games they will want to play as they grow up. It is also easier, I believe, so long as you are willing to be playful, get down on the ground, and focus on delighting the child.

Amusements and Games

In this book I loosely make a distinction between amusements and games. Amusements are like Peek-a-Boo or tossing your child up in the air; they are much simpler than games and usually involve basic cause and effect actions or acrobatics. But one key thing all amusements have in common is this: **something remarkable happens**. For example, when you have a closed fist and they try to open

See the International Foundation for Original Play at https://originalplay.eu

it, it doesn't just open, it turns into a creature and walks or it explodes like a firecracker. Such are amusements; they are simple, non-competitive, and generally result in a moment's delight.

Games, however, have more structure, ranging from simple to complex. They are generally competitive and involve skill, strategy, and chance. When you play with babies, you are playing amusements. As your children grow and develop, games emerge and eventually become the majority of what you play together.

Amusements	Games
Simple	Range from simple to complex
Basic cause and effect structure	3-part game arc structure (see Chapter 9)
Goal is to delight	Goal is the fulfillment of overcoming a challenge
Non-competitive	Often competitive
No rules needed	Rules generally needed
Often include acrobatics	Usually involve skill, strategy, and chance
Short duration (seconds to minutes)	Can be much longer
Can be appropriate for all ages	Not really suited for babies and some toddlers

The Goal is to Delight

Amusements carve gameplay down to the purest forms of play, for at the heart of every game is an amusement. I believe this simplification works best when there is a selfless focus on delighting your child. Hence the "fun" is not necessarily mutual or balanced in amusements; your enjoyment will be in delighting your child—hearing her laugh uncontrollably and begging for more.

Tips on tickling children

- Your instinct will probably be to really dig into them to maximize their laughter; however, not all kids like this. Start gently. With a well-timed anticipation, you might even get them to laugh uncontrollably by only implying that your hand is going to tickle them.
- Your instinct will also probably be to go after their armpits or the soles of their feet; however, I recommend the abdomen (i.e. belly, chest, sides of ribs).
- In terms of force and duration, a good principle is to use just less than what you think is enough. Two short tickle sessions that leave the child wanting more are better than one long session that leaves the kids feeling uncomfortable.
- The goal of tickling is to communicate "I got you and I love you", not "I win." A "tickle-kiss" is a great way to do this.

The Difference Between Fun and Delight

At a conversational level, "fun" and "delight" seem interchangeable. However, I do make a distinction between the two:

- Fun is a sense of enjoyment one step above satisfaction. It is a reflection on an experience that was entertaining and fulfilling, such as when the result of a game is even better than what you expected.
- Delight is a brief emotional elation, and it usually makes us laugh or even happily scream out of sudden excitement.

So while the feeling of spinning around quickly is delightful, a well-structured game that involves spinning is fun. Or put another way, it is fun to play Ticklebugs, because being tickled is a delight.

Types of Delight

In Part 1 of this book I describe the classification I use for all of our best impromptu games and amusements, which is organized not by name or date, but by what I believe the primary delight for the child is. While it is not an exhaustive categorization or one that will apply to all ages and cultures, it has worked well for the collection of games we have played.

These archetypes of delight, which seem to surface the most for my kids, can be seen in the outermost layers of the following sunburst diagram. There is also a whole category dedicated to what I call the "simple delights," such as being surprised, kissed, or briefly smushed. Being aware of these various types of delights will help you incorporate a good mix when you are crafting your own amusements.

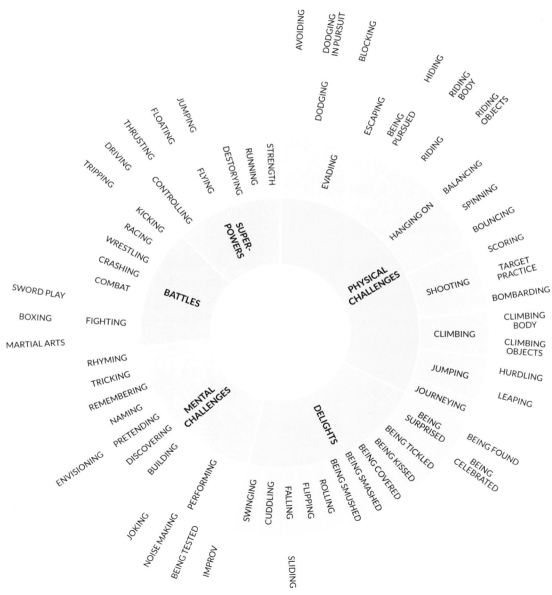

The Relationship Between Trust, Control, and Delight

I have found that for most amusements, a child's sense of control and her delight are almost inversely related, meaning that as she trustingly gives up control to you, her delight increases, and as that delight naturally declines, she regains composure and control.

You can see this by breaking down an amusement into phases:

1. The child begins in a state of self-control.
2. The amusement begins.
3. The child, in trusting you, subconsciously submits more and more control to you, awaiting something remarkable.
4. Something remarkable does happen, and the child relinquishes more control as the effect of the delight kicks in (e.g. laughing).
5. Delight peaks and then begins to wane as the child begins to regain composure.
6. The child returns to her original state of self-control.

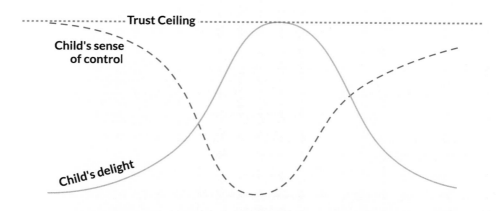

SELF-CONTROL		AWAITING		DELIGHT	COMPOSURE	SELF-CONTROL
1	2	3	4	5		6

This is the ideal state, where the child trusts you, yields control to you, and takes delight in the amusement. However, if the child does not trust you, that trust level acts like a ceiling, above which the level of delight cannot climb.

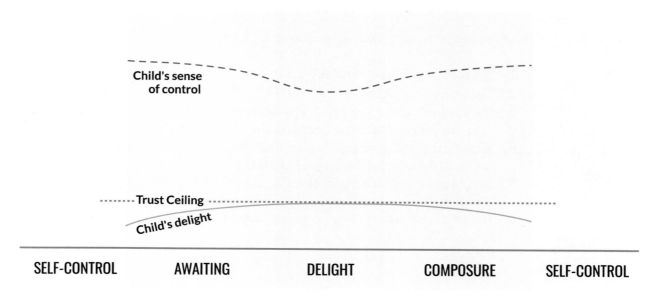

The point is that if the child does not trust you, and thus does not feel comfortable submitting control to you, that will inhibit her ability to take delight in the amusement. If you go to a friend's house and play with their kids (who do not know you that well), do not start with amusements that involve acrobatics or even touching. Welcome them in with age-appropriate amusements that establish yourself as trustworthy.

Interestingly enough, amusements in the superpowers category seem to be an exception to the trust-control-delight relationship. While a high level of trust is required for superpower amusements, the child's imagined sense of control is augmented far beyond what is realistic, and that is what delivers the delight. See Chapter 10 for several examples.

Structure of an Amusement

Let's take a close look at one of the most universal amusements, breaking down its structure so we can understand how it works.

Peek-a-boo

1. Peek-a-boo starts with you and a baby looking at each other.
2. You initiate the play by covering your face with your hands and saying the baby's name: "Where's Whitney?"
3. You pause briefly, while the baby watches and waits.
4. You open up your hands and look directly at the baby, saying in a happy voice, "There she is!"
5. The baby likely laughs at this and wants to do it again.
6. You might repeat this sequence multiple times.

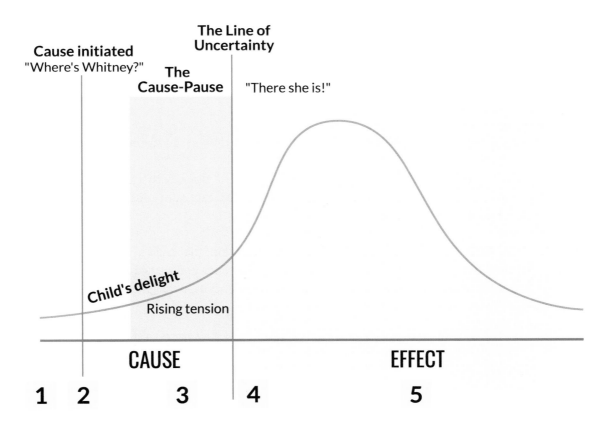

You can see that this amusement is composed of a cause and an effect, but there are a few more details worth noting. Let's take a look at each step:

- Step 1 is just the prerequisite of playing.
- Step 2 is the **cause**, which you control by initiating it.
- After the cause, there is a pause (step 3) that you control by determining its duration. This "**cause-pause**" must occur for at least three reasons:
  - to separate the cause and the effect, so they do not blur together
  - to allow the child time to cognitively develop an expectation of what is going to happen
  - to purposely intensify the tension, creating an emotional buildup that will be converted to delight
- The duration of the cause-pause is unclear to the child, and it ends as the **effect** begins (step 4). That boundary line is the "**line of uncertainty**."
- The baby's emotional response to the effect is (ideally) **delight** (step 5).
- As step 6 indicates, this can repeat for several iterations.

If you take a step back, you can see that steps 2 and 3 are the anticipation, and step 3 is the key ingredient of uncertainty. Tenacity, momentum, and the enlivening are also important ingredients of Peek-a-boo, but not nearly to the same degree.

Developing Amusements Through Iteration

You can repeat those same steps in Peek-a-boo several times with a baby and get the same result. But as the baby grows into a toddler, abundant repetition of the same amusement leads to boredom.

Intentionally injecting variety can not only maintain the child's interest but increase the level of delight. As a result, amusements are developed through iteration, not exact repetition. When this is done well, I call it a delight spiral.

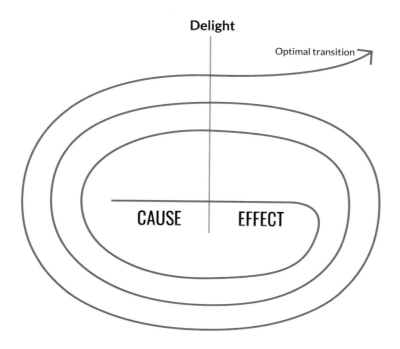

Delight

Optimal transition

CAUSE | EFFECT

Delight Spirals

Instead of repeating the same amusement in a loop, iterate on it in more of a spiral, seeking to reach a higher level of delight in each loop. This works best if you initiate the next iteration right before the child's delight level returns back to stasis.

Let's take a look at a real-world example: holding a fussy toddler in arm on hip.

Iteration 1
- Cause: Ready...Set...
    - Eye contact
    - Serious voice
    - Growing intensity
    - Kid says "Go"
- Effect: Jiggling up and down for 2-3 seconds
- You can repeat this iteration a couple of times.

Iteration 2
- Cause: RSG
- Effect: Jiggling and moving back and forth

Iteration 3
- Cause: RSG
- Effect: Jiggling and spinning

Iteration 4
- Cause: RSG
- Effect: Jiggling and dipping upside down

(continue with additional similar iterations)

You can see that for each iteration, a slightly different and ideally more exciting effect is used. You can repeat each iteration once or twice, but then you need to move on. Rarely do I "move back" to a previous iteration, though that can be done if you are running out of ideas or if you want to create a stronger contrast for an upcoming iteration.

The Power of Superpowers

Both kids and adults wish they had superpowers, but only kids suspect they actually have them. As adults we have long since let the reality of human limitations numb our suspicions of unique greatness; we cannot fly or run superfast or hear what's happening on the other side of the world, so we stop trying.

But the resilient hope of a child is demonstrated when, though constantly faced with limitations, she does not give up on there just possibly being a chance she has extraordinary abilities (like maybe I do become blurry when I run really fast). You have the power and imagination to temporarily grant your kids new abilities and suspend the limitations that make life seem so unfair.

Amusements of this kind (which I call superpowers) can be some of the easiest to create yet most fulfilling to play. I have found that superpower activities are ideal for the little ones (1-3 years old), for whom they seem especially magical.

Give child a fantastic ability, then let her experience it

Discovering Superpowers

The objective in creating a superpower amusement is to bestow a fantastic capability to your child, and then, through your own support and enlivening, let her fully experience it. Three methods I have used to do this include augmenting existing abilities, removing limitations, and creating new abilities.

Exaggerating abilities

The simplest way to do this is to just add the word "super" to the front of whatever verb your kid does and then enact what that would look like. This is by far the most common method I use.

Running	Super runs (Now she can run much faster)
Jumping	Super Jumps (Now she can jump much higher and farther)

You can also choose to then generalize the action into a broader, thematic ability, allowing for more creative examples of the superpower's use.

Existing ability	Jumping
Exaggerated ability	Super Jumps
Thematic superpower	Ninja stunt abilities
Superpower activity	Parkour

Removing limitations

A similar way to look at this is that you are removing things that confine the child to reality. The end result is the same as an exaggerated ability, but how you arrived at it is different.

This can arise naturally by just playing along with a child's creative ideas. For example, if the child runs up to you, holds onto your leg, and pretends to lift you, the reality is that she is not going to be able to lift you. But it is magical for her to see you rise off the ground with your arms flailing (i.e. Super Strength), because she discovers in playing with you that she can do what she thought was only pretend in her own mind.*

Another way to remove limitations is by "forgetting" established or assumed rules. There is a good reason you have a rule to not jump on the couch, but sometimes there can be a waiver in the name of play.

Limitation	No making messes
Superpower	Massively destructive abilities unleashed
Superpower activity	Destructo

New Abilities

A third perspective on creating superpowers is that you are creating novel, preposterous abilities that have wondrous impact. These can take the form of "what if..." logic.

For example, you could think of how a child's mundane activity could be ten times awesomer.

- Going up the stairs >> Flying
- Pushing a button on my leg turns me into a monster (Monster Button)

Or you could find ways of combining abilities into superabilities. In my experience though, it is more effective to exaggerate a single ability and focus your efforts on enlivening a theme.

Your child always has superpowers

Superpower activities become a common way of playing for us. When I would look at my child and genuinely try to "make things awesome" for her, the result was usually a superpower activity. And if one superpower started to lose its power through overuse, it was relatively easy to find another superpower to replace it. I looked at it as though my kids always had superpowers, and I just got to select which ones were turned on.

This non-verbal way of saying "yes" to the child's playful suggestion is a great example of creative kindness.

Having a noble purpose

I believe that deep down almost everyone wants to be a hero and thus wants an opportunity to be brave. More advanced superpower activities can provide your child the opportunity to trial out their powers for good. You can support that by enacting an antagonist in a playful, non-scary way, which begins to transition superpower activities from amusements into games.

Amusements are wonderful for their simplicity and can be created by focusing on abundant anticipation and uncertainty. They can even be simplified versions of games. Creating good games, however, requires a bit more explanation, and that is the focus of the next chapter.

SCENARIO: Questions to ask when you want your child to put on his pajamas for bedtime

UNPLAYFUL
What, you still don't have your pajamas on? What have you been doing all this time?

PLAYFUL
Did you know that zombies cannot see you if you have pajamas on? Wait a minute, are those zombies I hear coming this way...?

CHAPTER 9

Designing Impromptu Games

The previous chapter analysed amusements, which by their simplicity tend to have a fairly common structure. This chapter analyzes games, which by their very nature are more intricate, and thus more varied. In analyzing the wide variety of games we have played, I have not found a universal game structure that simply fits them all, but I do see several common patterns and attributes that make games more enjoyable. So as you explore play with your kids, use this chapter not as a prescriptive formula but as an outline for pairing good ingredients.

Gamifying Amusements

As my children have grown in size and age, so have our amusements grown into games. Amusements can evolve into games by gently introducing game elements like simple rules, competition, or a challenging goal. The primary way I gamify amusements is by adding tensity.

Tiered Tensity

Since amusements are not focused on skill or strategy, amusement tensity is more about controlling the degree of excitement, perhaps by how wild the movements are. As you gamify amusements, you slowly change the nature and amount of tensity by first introducing a simple challenge framed by basic rules.

Here is a real-life example of creating a simple game from one of our favorite amusements: Super Jumping.

Step 1: Start with an amusement

In Super Jumping, I direct where the child goes, and I fully assist in getting the child there. In other words, he is just having a great time hanging on.

Step 2: Establish a theme by adding a mission

As the fun of Super Jumping starts to wane, instead of transitioning to a different amusement, I introduce a mission.

- We sit down on his toddler bed, I grab his favorite stuffed animal, and I toss it to the other side of the room, saying that we need to "save the bunny!"
- That is not quite enough information to make the objective clear, so I toss a couple of pillows on the ground and say, "Quick, jump on these stones, but whatever you do, don't step in the carpet lava."
- We then do super jumps on the stones, reach down and grab the bunny, and then jump back to the safety of his bed.

Throughout this process, I am still directing where we jump to, and I am fully assisting him in getting there. The only difference now is that there is a story forming, and I am providing the scaffolding of how to achieve that goal.

Step 3: Iteratively Add Tensity

A mission is not the same thing as tensity, but it becomes a basis for adding tensity. You can add tensity (i.e. make the mission harder) in a variety of ways, including:

- Removing scaffolding
  - Add decision autonomy (e.g. by letting him choose where to go next)
  - Reduce physical assistance (e.g. by only holding on to one hand instead of two)
- Layering on additional challenges

- Add task complexity (e.g. by creating more steps to the mission, more adversaries)
- Add rules/limitations (e.g. can only step on each stone once, have a time limit)

I find it more intuitive to add tensity by first establishing a story or game theme. This also gives you a foundation for adding the enlivening. However, make sure not to add all the tensity at once, lest you overwhelm the child. Tensity should be tiered so that each iteration is only slightly more complex or difficult than the previous one. It is similar to delight spirals but with tensity being the main factor. This iterative process teaches the child about game structure and sets him up to be successful at having fun.

Additionally, I have found that, even though the goal of an amusement is to delight the child, there is plenty of opportunity to challenge the limits of your own creativity by devising the next interesting and skill-appropriate challenge for the child that fits into the story-theme of the game.

Common Attributes of Games

Games are more complex than amusements because the goal in a game is the fulfillment of overcoming a challenge, not just experiencing a delight. What that means is that games often exhibit additional attributes that surround a central amusement, including:
- a three-part game arc structure
- skill, strategy, and chance
- competition between multiple players
- rules that balance tensity

The Game Arc

There are complicated textbooks out there on game systems and game design, but I do not think you need to understand all of that to create fun impromptu games with your kids. I found a simpler, more intuitive analogy to be more applicable.

When I stepped back and analyzed the games my kids and I play, I saw that the process of facing and overcoming a challenge in a game is consistent with the pattern found in good stories. Games and stories have a similar structure in that they have a beginning, middle, and end and the order and function of each part matters. You might have seen the story arc before, which can be applied to practically every story ever told.

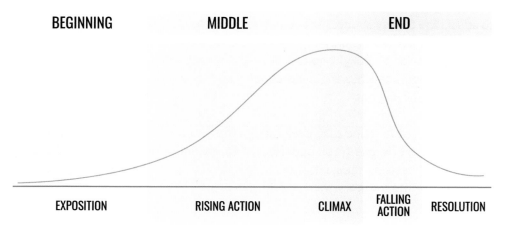

The games I have constructed with my kids follow a similar pattern, boiling down to having three corresponding parts: an expectation, a complication, and a fulfillment.

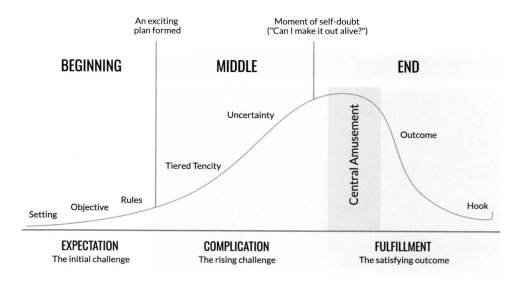

The Expectation

The expectation sets up the game so everyone knows what to do. It consists of three parts: the setting, the objective, and rules. With the right mixture of those parts, the expectation should result in each player having an exciting plan for what is about to happen. There should be an initial feeling of confidence, where each player thinks he can see what will happen, even though it is uncertain.

While the expectation is an important part of the game arc, it can also be the most boring. I have found that the ideal format to aim for is an **implied expectation** (rather than explicit verbal delivery), where the child deduces what to do by leveraging familiar patterns from other games you play together and from basic human psychology. Before we discuss how, let's look at the main parts of the expectation in more detail.

Setting

Though required in stories, I find I rarely use or embellish setting in games, choosing instead to leave it up to the child's imagination. In Frog and the Log, the game is still fun even if they are not imagining that they are in a forest and that you are a log and they are a frog.

Some games need more information about the "where" and "when" of the game so that the child can better immerse himself and respond in a way that makes sense. In those cases, keep the setting information brief and enticing, as in Crown of Splendor, where the anticipation statement ("I am the king, this is my kingdom, and I sit on my throne") is all the setting context needed, and since it is said in a silly, dramatic voice, it does not come across as mundane information.

Asteroids also has a setting-based anticipation statement ("Deep in space...there are..."), because everything about that game has a space theme. But note that that is all the information given; you do not even need to say that you are in a spaceship or on some kind of a mission. You can of course provide extra descriptive information for purposes of the enlivening (planets you are zooming by, galaxies in the distance, etc.), but that keeps the child waiting for the exciting parts, so I only do so sparingly or for a caesura effect. Instead, focus on the enlivening itself (e.g. make the asteroids feel real through sound effects).

If you think of the game as a story, the plot will be the exciting part worth focusing on, so for most games with young kids, you can either imply a setting without saying anything (e.g. a Ticklebug crawling at you communicates plenty), leverage an anticipation statement with some enlivening (e.g. Lifeboat's "All aboard!"), or skip it altogether.

Objective

This is the initial challenge the child is up against, which should be both interesting and intuitive. I like to make sure the objective goes far beyond what they get to do in "real life," like wrestle a blind monster or steal a crown right off of a king's head. Objectives that merely test a specific skill, like seeing how high the child can jump, are short-lived, lack the intrigue that motivates one to engage, and thus lead to brief, if any, fun.

By saying the objective should be intuitive, I mean that, even though it is a vital part of the expectation, ideally you do not have to spend any time explaining it. In Asteroids, the objective is to avoid space debris, and that is fairly intuitive when an asteroid is flying right at you. And in Ooga Booga, well, what would you do if a wild caveman came running at you?

Simple Rules

Most games will need some limitations put on the players to confine them to an engaging place where they must overcome the challenge. In Asteroids, you need to stay sitting; running away changes the game into something else, especially for the player sending the asteroids. Without rules, the game can break down in unsatisfying ways, such as when tensity is unbalanced between players.

Realistically, younger children will only retain one or maybe two rules, so if you need to have rules, start with one main one and add more later. And even though older children can handle more rules, try to express them concisely, perhaps in two or four words each.

I also find that I use a different voice when I am imparting rules. The voice I use for the anticipation and enlivening is purposely dramatic and dynamic, invoking attention and excitement. But the instruction voice is a very clear, calm, normal voice, which indirectly communicates that there is a seriousness and importance to what is being said.

Implied Expectations

It is worth noting that the majority of the games we play have essentially no preamble (other than the anticipation). The very first time you play a game, you might need to state a clear objective and rules for there to be an effective expectation. Subsequently, however, it can be redundant to reiterate them. In fact, for most simple games, there never was a point where we talked about objectives and rules. Sleeping Giant is literally the result of me being tired, lying on the ground, and my kids jumping around on me enough that I realized I might as well make it fun and chase them. No setting was necessary (I named it "Sleeping Giant" later on), the objective is clearly to avoid getting caught, and there aren't really any rules. Looking back, I believe that is the ideal setup for impromptu games with young kids.

So why then even consider an expectation when designing impromptu games? As your kids grow, the expectation becomes a more vital (though still brief) part of the game experience, because it prevents disparities that lead to broken play (e.g. kids mistakenly running away from you instead of at you in Juggernaut). Additionally, playful children will routinely change up a game with their own silly ideas (e.g. Cage That Animal can start with escaping a zookeeper and then morph into a series of funny animal pantomimes). That should be encouraged, but since they might do it without regard for if that will break the play for others or be an interesting challenge, you will need to rapidly evaluate the emerging expectation to see if it leads to an exciting plan or not.

The Complication

In fairy tales, no stroll through the woods is uneventful. After the child embarks with an exciting plan, he encounters surprising complications. At this stage of the game, a *rising challenge* emerges. It is not necessarily the same as the objective's initial challenge, for this time it is not obvious to the child if he will be able to overcome it. The result of the complication is a moment of self-doubt, when the child is not sure he will achieve the desired outcome after all. I believe the figurative question in the child's mind is, "Can I make it out alive?" (**CIMIOA**).

The main parts of the complication are some of the same ones that make gameplay fun: tensity and uncertainty. Throughout this stage, tensity increases, usually in a tiered manner, pushing and stretching the child. However, the tensity needs to be balanced so that by working harder to overcome the challenge, he is building up a feeling of accomplishment (rather than discouragement or boredom), which makes the game's outcome more fulfilling.

Uncertainty is what makes the complication surprising and, like manipulation of interest, shows the child that there is more here than he thought there would be in the expectation. In terms of timing, you need to introduce the complication just before the child is ready for it, before he has mastered the initial challenge; otherwise, boredom can get a foothold and disrupt the play. Uncertainty also can help balance the tensity between players, as randomness is the agent of chance and luck.

Impromptu games are a lot more interesting when there is not just an objective and rules, like in most sports, but a distinct initial challenge and rising challenge, which is the complication. I have seen at least four main types of complications emerge in the games we play: natural consequences, amplifications, variations, and new dimensions.

GAME	INITIAL CHALLENGE	RISING CHALLENGE	COMPLICATION TYPE
Sleeping Giant	Wake the giant	Escape from running giant	Natural Consequences
Statue of Limitations	Steal special item from statue	Escape from running statue	Natural Consequences
Shinobi	Deflect incoming blocks	Deflect faster, rapid-fire blocks	Amplification
GoGo Juice	Wrestle slow Daddy	Escape from superfast Daddy	Amplification
Asteroids	Avoid asteroids	Avoid cosmic rays, aliens, etc.	Variation
DodgeArm	Avoid head attacks	Avoid assorted attacks/combos	Variation
Tripwire	Jump over wire	Jump over moving wire	New Dimension
Beware the Lightning	Jump past lightning	Jump past moving lightning	New Dimension

Natural Consequences

This is the most analogous to the story metaphor, for as the child appears to overcome the initial challenge, he discovers a new, bigger, and more urgent challenge arising as a direct result of his actions. The objective of the game actually changes. If you can steal the crown from the king in Crown of Splendor, you better start running.

Amplification

In this case, as the child is just about to master the initial challenge, it evolves, and he must face a bigger, faster, stronger version of the same challenge. In Blind Monster Wrestling, I usually start out slowly, with a lot more growling and swiping than actual hunting. As the game progresses, I am rapidly rolling around and diving in almost random directions. Amplification pushes the child into higher levels of required skill.

Variation

In this case, as the child is just about to master the initial challenge, similar challenges arise that might only be slightly different. Ticklebugs is a great example, where the pattern of attack is a stream of a variety of creatures, each with its own personality and strengths. In Asteroids, the complication is the series of bombardments of not only faster asteroids (amplification), but gamma rays, wormholes, aliens, and other types of surprising space encounters—all coming at different speeds and trajectories. Variation requires extra creativity, but it leads to silly moments and fun memories.

New Dimensions

In this case, as the child is just about to master the initial challenge, the very nature of the challenge changes, requiring the child to solve problems in new ways using new tactics. This is a bit of a combination of the other three types of complications. In Beware the Lighting, avoiding stationary lighting is relatively easy, but then it starts to move around, introducing the notion of pattern recognition and timing.

The Fulfillment

While the expectation ended with a false sense of confidence and the complication ended with a false sense of doubt (the CIMIOA moment), the fulfillment brings a true conclusion that resolves the built-up physical and emotional tension.

The Central Amusement

Its cornerstone, and the climax of the entire game, is the central amusement that is embedded in the game. The result of the amusement is delight, which in basic games might be a fun movement, such as flying, falling, or even inertia. In chasing games, this can be the tickling and kissing. In skill games, this can be a personal best or even a retry. The delight also has the function of ushering in the game's outcome.

The Outcome

Just as a story has an ending that resolves the plot, games need an outcome to provide a satisfying conclusion to the challenge of the complication. In chasing games, the outcome for the child is generally to be caught. In sports and other competitive games, it is one team winning. You can control the outcome to treat it as a penalty or reward (for example, if the child is cheating or if the child needs assistance). This should be done sparingly, though, so that you do not turn into a Game Bully.

The key thing about the outcome is that it is not the key thing; focus your efforts on having a great central amusement with a cathartic delight. The outcome is more of a transitional element, leading to the hook.

The Hook

The hook is what you use to actually do the transition to the next level, a new game, or the end of playtime. It is essentially the first step of the next game, just like a hook in a story might be the first sentence of the book. In Cage That Animal, the outcome is that the zookeeper returns the animal to the cage, but then the zookeeper turns his back, opening an opportunity for the animal to escape, starting up the game again. That is the hook.

One other thing to consider about the game arc is that, since the fun of gameplay should be mutual, it also applies to the adult. The dual nature of the game arc means you have your own expectation (e.g. chase the kid), complication (e.g. wow

GAME	AMUSEMENT	DELIGHT	OUTCOME	HOOK
Sleeping Giant	Escaping giant	Tickle-kiss	Caught by the giant	Attention to other child
Ooga Booga	Escaping caveman	Tickle-hug/kiss	Caught by caveman	Space to hear "Ooga booga"
No Fun for Anyone	Escaping mean lady	Tossed on couch	Caught by mean lady	She turns her back
Blind Monster Wrestling	Avoiding monster	Tickle-kiss	"Devoured" by beast	Monster snarls again
Asteroids	Deflecting asteroids	Tickle	Caught in black hole	Another asteroid flies by
Shoops	Shooting	Scoring	Basket filled	Switch baskets
Boom the Castle	Shooting at castle	Knock down castle	King knocked over	New castle being built
Food Guy	Coming up with different food items	Funny enactments and chasing	Get full and lie down	Next person becomes the food guy

that kiddo is surprisingly agile), and fulfillment (e.g. hearing the uncontrollable laughter of your child). Several of the games in Part 1 include a description of these phases of the game arc for the child and for the adult.

Skill, Strategy, and Chance

The primary factors of game tensity are skill, strategy, and chance. Some combination of these are required to make it fun to overcome the challenge in a game.

Skill

Skill is an ability or knowledge needed to accomplish a goal. Games that require skill expect a certain level of capability from the child, which can result in a somewhat blunt "pass-fail" mentality. As such, I recommend not relying on skill alone in skill-based games (e.g. incorporate strategy and chance). Additionally, use a tiered approach in skill-based games, such as starting close to the goal and moving farther back if that is too easy. In general, one-on-one sports games like Shoops or Trampoline Soccer tend to be skill-focused, and while that simplicity can work well with small children, it can also quickly become discouraging for them, so either use those as skill-building practices (rather than competitions), or make sure you balance tensity with unequal rules or by similar means.

Also, be aware that **skill** (what you can do) is not the same as **performance** (what you did do), as some kids will have off days or be too excited to make a clutch shot. Encouragement and grace are important to model here, with the goal of shaping character, improving future performances, and enhancing the overall play experience.

Strategy

You use strategy in a game when you plan a path to success. It is in how you use your ability and knowledge (i.e. skill) to achieve the goal. Strategy provides an intellectual avenue that does not necessarily require prerequisite abilities or knowledge. While strategy becomes a major part of games with older kids, it can be very satisfying for a small child to discover a new strategy (even if it seems obvious to you). Try to require strategy in games without having a single or obvious solution. In Beware the Lighting, for example, it can be surprising how the youngest children find a path through even the hardest obstacles.

Chance

Chance is what makes the outcome of a game unpredictable. Especially in skill-based games, it is important to have a counteracting force of luck to balance the tensity and maintain mutual fun. In Blind Monster Wrestling, I sometimes dive out in random directions, for if they are not there, they laugh about how far off I am, while if they are there, I just happened to get a break in catching them. In other games, creating chance can be more difficult. I usually start with contrived disabilities (like the blindness in Blind Monster Wrestling) and motivating my kids to be bold in taking calculated risks (e.g. shooting a long shot or running through a small hole), for those lead to interesting opportunities for surprising results.

Player Arrangements

Games have players, who work with, against, or alongside each other. There are a variety of ways to organize players and teams, so when creating a game, do not just default to one standard way.

Player Arrangements when Playing with One Child

Even when it is just you and one child, there are at least three ways to set up teams.

Dad as Opponent

When I play with one of my children, I am often assuming an opponent role, like in Juggernaut or Crown of Splendor. Note that it is not an anonymous role (it is an actual, worthy opponent), and I am not playing as "Daddy" (except for sport games like Trampoline Soccer and Basketballoon). In some games, who the main opponent is can just be left ambiguous, like in Narco Polo, because it is immaterial to the game.

Dad as Facilitator

More often than not though, I serve as the game's theme object, functioning more as an action facilitator than an opponent. In Timber, I am the tree. In Lifeboat, I am the boat. In Asteroids, I am the asteroids. In Beware the Lightning, I am the lightning.

Dad and Child as Team

It is a lot of mutual fun to be on the same team as your child, working toward the same goal, like in Shoops where you are both trying to fill the basket with blocks. This can be challenging to implement when playing with just one child if there is not an external object to work against (e.g. you cannot be the asteroids and participate in avoiding the asteroids).

Player Arrangements when Playing with Multiple Children

When you are playing with multiple children, multiple new permutations arise.

All Against One

This usually takes the form of either all against Daddy or all against a foe (usually played by Daddy). It is not so much that the "all" is a team, but rather a collection of individuals all trying to stay in the game against a common opponent. Backwards Tag is a good example.

Each One Against All

This might be a useful arrangement to consider, but we almost never used the "every man for himself" arrangement, except for experimenting with different types of tag.

Teams

The more kids there are, the more useful teams become. Whether you are a player on a team or a neutral facilitator, you should be the one to assign teams, as it allows you to balance tensity and protect children with more delicate self-esteems. If the kids are really competitive or emotional, I opt for turn-taking instead.

Turn-Taking

As long as the game moves along quickly, with lots of iterations of play, I find kids cooperate very well with turn-taking. This is also what I use when there are too many children to play safely (e.g. Blind Monster Wrestling). You can have individuals take turns (with the rest in an orderly line) or have squads take turns (i.e. a group of kids that cycle in together to play).

Creating Good Rules

Good rules will balance tensity by confining players to a space where interesting performances happen. If you are confined in a cage with a blind monster, you cannot just avoid the conflict by running far away. Rules help eliminate the short-cuts that can abruptly end a game before the fulfillment phase.

As discussed earlier, work to keep game rules simple, universal, and concise. Avoid detailed stipulations that only apply to certain players in certain situations (i.e. the folly of the Game Lawyer). Rules should be used to maintain momentum (e.g. create time limits if turns are taking too long), and you should only create rules if you have to, as explaining them bloats the expectation phase, slowing things down. There is always a need, however, for implied rules of conduct, such as no hurting one another and no bullying, though these too are likely only specified when necessary.

On Winning and Learning

We have a phrase in my family, which my wife and I like to use when we compete against each other: We win! It reminds us that we are ultimately on the same team, that we should be quick to encourage and affirm one another, and that there are no losers in win-win situations. Having that mentality, I look for the game's outcome to always be a winning scenario for the child. She can win by succeeding (e.g. with a proud reward, like when I lift her on my shoulders and cheer at her personal best) or win by losing (e.g. with a happy penalty, like getting sucked into the black hole in Asteroids). Either way, she "wins" with a good experience.

So if each game goes through a game arc with a fulfillment that is "guaranteed," then losing is not such a bad thing, because it can be fun. As a result, to me the notion of losing is really more about learning: refining skills and devising new strategies to achieve an outcome. And when we try our best and still fail, to not be crushed by it but move forward honorably and cheerfully. These are life-long skills we all need, and each game played is an opportunity to work on them.

CHAPTER 10
Improvisation

Freedom to Experiment

Thus far, my analysis of play with my kids has probably made you assume you need to apply just the right set of calculated features at just the right timing for play to be fun for your kids. But that is not at all how I actually play with my kids, so I do not recommend you do that either. Though having a plan of what you will play is valuable, most of the work and decision-making actually happens moment by moment during play (hence the importance of the continuous feedback loop).

My approach in playing with my kids is more like an experiment than a formula. I am always trying out some variation of things to discover new fun amusements and to keep things fresh and interesting for my kids. To do so requires a steady supply of both play opportunities and creativity, as well as a willingness to embrace imperfect or untried ideas.

Whether or not you feel you are a creative person when put on the spot, the techniques in this chapter will help you discover new games and ways to have fun together. I think improvisation is almost a required ingredient of impromptu play with your kids, taking the form of a befitting enlivening and an ever-evolving plan for the gameplay.

Discovering a Creative Enlivening

Most of the creative improvisation I do involves discovering a new, better, more creative enlivening than whatever my default plan was going to be. It is needed when I portray a character (e.g. opponent, creature) or am acting in the theme or story of the game (e.g. space, jungle, deep sea).

Portrayal

By portrayal I am referring to acting. While I have not studied acting, I have learned by playing with my kids that I primarily use three means of representing something dramatically:

- **Voice**: Such as enlivening voices and sound effects
- **Body movement**: Such as my actions, my posture, and my facial expressions
- **Timing**: Such as using dramatic pauses and changing the speed of my movements

Each one of these is like a fun-multiplier in the enlivening, so use all three—pretty much at all times. And for anyone thinking, "Well, that's just not my thing," be encouraged in knowing that the quality of the portrayal almost does not matter. Just attempting it communicates the playful intention that invites the child in. It is all the more effective though if you are willing to go "all in" and make it feel real.

Tips about Portrayal

Everything needs sound effects

This is part of your role and a major part of the enlivening. I find that when I am playing with my kids, I am either talking in one of the enlivening voices (such as the Squier Crier or Vicarious Exclamations) or making sound effects for the various actions or creatures; silence is rare, though I sometimes use it for a caesura effect before I rebuild momentum.

Exaggerate portrayal to be obvious

At its core, the enlivening is a way of communicating with your child. And just as you should not mumble when you speak, it is best to make the enlivening obvious by adding a bit more emotion and movement than you would initially think is enough. Just make sure that it is for the child's benefit and not your own, the folly of the Game Clown. It also helps to focus the child's attention to one thing at a time.

There are no straight lines

Straight lines are more predictable and less interesting than curves and paths that change direction. When chasing my kids, I do not merely follow right behind them:

- I chart a path that might cut them off up ahead
- Or I almost grab them, but then suddenly go silent and disappear
- Or I take great zig-zag bounds and try to scare them with loud approaching foot stomps

The same is true with bodily movements. Unless you are trying to portray a robot, move your body with grand, fluid, curved motions, starting with your eyes, then your face, then your body, then your arms. There is a gracefulness to it with imbued emotion.

"Imitate what you imaginate"

I am a fairly visual person, so it helps to see something in my mind before I try to portray it. I do this by slipping into the story of the game, imagining more about it or what would happen next, and then translating that into my own actions. Except when trying to do something random, I need to imagine it first and stay one step ahead.

Change your elevation

Especially with younger children, it is a good practice to communicate with your kids at their eye level. Use that as a starting point in the game, and from there you can lie down, crawl, or hunch. Fresh ideas can come from starting in a different position with a different perspective.

Tips about Timing

Don't ask questions

While I encourage you to co-create with your kids by being open and accepting of their ideas, don't do it by asking lots of questions. That slows down the momentum and is a characteristic of the Game Wimp. Instead, be bold and press ahead with your next action, even though it might be ambiguous.

Fill in the gaps

Use the naturally occurring pauses in a game as opportunities for creativity. When a child starts laughing, she is also watching you for the next funny thing you will do. When a child is tired and stops for a moment to rest, or is looking back to see if you are following her, you have the spotlight to creatively advance the play. Her pauses are a time for you to be "on."

Be spontaneous

Don't wait for your kids to ask. Don't wait for your kids to finish laughing. Don't wait for certainty on the best next step. Don't wait for the game to end to decide on what is next.

Tips about Creativity

Name the game

Naming each game you create with your kids forces you to establish and stick to a theme. From there you can direct your improvisation to embellish that theme.

Distinction avoids confusion

Especially with variations, do not try to be subtle. In Ticklebugs, I try to create unique creatures with extreme differences. The result might appear only slight, but aiming for distinction minimizes potential confusion. If you have similar-looking variations, you might need to inject distinction by naming them. For example, in Asteroids, if the next item is going to be a gamma ray or an X-ray, I often resort to calling it out, so the child is less likely to get frustrated.

Silly is better than normal, which is better than dead air

Perhaps it goes without saying, but when playing with your kids, it is better to be playful than serious. As you are searching for ideas and ridiculous ones come to mind, your kids might actually like those better than the practical ones you thought were better. So do not get stuck (i.e. dead air) in the process of de-crazing ideas or by setting a high practicality bar. Creativity is limitless, though filled with impractical and inconvenient ideas. For example, a sandwich shop has a finite number of toppings you can put on a sandwich, but when you play Sandwich, there is no limit to the silly types of things you could put on it.

"You want unicorn glitter on your sandwich?
Well it just so happens I have a bottle of that right here..."

There can be magic in anything

If you need the game to change and need help looking for ideas, create your own miracle by figuratively tapping your magic wand on something, giving it special powers that only make sense in the world of imaginative play.

"Yes and" your kids

The classic improv example of maintaining momentum is to accept your partner's idea and further develop it by saying, "Yes, and..." It is not all on you to think everything up; co-create with your kids. Your kids will likely come up with the silliest, most random, most ridiculously creative ideas. Do your best to say, "Yes," when your kids want to play and "Yes, and..." when they share their ideas.

Exploring for Variations

Game variations seem to just naturally emerge when you are creatively playing with your kids, though sometimes you might want to proactively invoke a change. Here are a few techniques that help you do that.

Changing One Key Variable

Looking back at how all our various games came about, I see that the main approach I used in exploring variations of games was to think about a single variable and then change it. There are lots of potential variables you can use, and generally changing just one is enough to make a variation feel like a whole new game. Here are some examples from the games we have played:

- Change location: Soccer in the trampoline
- Change speed: Slow-motion chase
- Change sides: First I lift you up, now you lift me up

- Change the reference: Thor's Hammer vs Hulk Punches
- Change the weapon/main object: By the Bolts of Zeus vs By the Balloon of Zeus
- Change the goal/target: Shoops vs Whiteboard Shoops
- Change projected personality: Poke of Death vs Weevil-Rat-Worm
- Change implied environment: Ticklebugs vs Ticklefish
- Change the cause's effect: Poke Music vs Monster Button

Math as a Method for Innovation

Once you have identified a variable, there are several different ways you can modify it. As a product designer, I often do a lot of "what if" thought experiments that usually follow basic mathematical operations as a way of finding new combinations and ideas. This technique can also be applied in devising new games.

Addition

Like addition, you can create something new by adding in a totally different element. A good example of this is when you create amusement combinations, where you enhance an amusement by combining it with another amusement. For example, Climbing the Coconut Tree is a lot of fun, but you can take it to a whole new level if you combine it with spinning.

Subtraction

Or like subtraction, you can remove something from the game, such as when you remove a key rule or object. What would soccer be like without a ball? Perhaps you will discover a pantomime game that is less about competition and more about demonstrating what the most amazing scoring kick looks like.

Multiplication and Division

When you only adjusting a variable (rather than adding or removing it), you can think about it as multiplying or dividing that factor. This is a great way to turn up the action. What would soccer be like with two balls instead of one? GoGo Juice uses huge fluctuations in speed to create essentially different modes in the game (turbo vs slow motion). Most superpowers, like Super Jumping and Super Runs, are like applying multiplication, while contrived disabilities, like slow motion or playing while on your knees, can be thought of as using division.

When you get stuck in a lackluster game, these mathematical operators are a memorable way of finding a unique twist that gives the game new life.

Ideation Based on the Child's Preferences

If you feel you need something more specific, I recommend focusing on the child and what she likes (e.g. castles). Start with something generic and then identify a more specific component of that (e.g. castles have flags at the top). Then incorporate that into the set of objects from the existing game and see if there is an interesting variable to swap. It might take a few trials, but this technique has the potential benefit of being more thoughtful.

Ideation Using Your Environment

If you are still struggling to come up with a unique idea for how to mutate a game, you can always look and listen around you in that moment for ideas. Pick a random point and fixate briefly on something there.

- Is there an object there that you can use?
  - e.g. a rope, a ball, a pile of leaves, a broom
- Is there an attribute about what you are looking at that leads to an idea?
  - e.g. the hose is leaking > wet > play the game with the sprinklers on
- Is there an action related to what you are looking at that leads to an idea?
  - e.g. hear a dog bark > barking > play the game as a loud animal

Improv in Mental Challenge Games

Songs and Rhyming

Improvising songs is one of the most challenging types of improv for me since there are so many different creative parts that need to come together well for it to be effective. In Sing Me a Song, I often get stuck trying to come up with a good melody, but I have learned by observing my wife improv that it is way more effective to just pick a familiar song and replace its words. If you are trying to avoid parody, you can pick a song your kids would not know. Either way, focus more on the words, and if you are creating your own melody, it is okay to just have a basic line and intro beat.

A similar technique can be used when searching for a good rhyme. You can use a limerick or another familiar pattern. And in terms of length, just a basic couplet could be enough, either as two phrases or broken into four lines (e.g. ABCB). Additionally, work backwards by figuring out the best word and saving that for the punchline at the end of the song. Then find a word that rhymes with that and use that in the first half of the rhyme.

Random Objects

Generating random objects might be your most useful improv tool, and several techniques for doing that have already been described earlier in this chapter. However, you cannot use purely random things when playing with your kids. You need to apply a quick filter to make sure they are appropriate and things your child would be familiar with. It is even better, though, if you can take a seemingly random object and apply it meaningfully to the story of the game. I try to find ways of connecting such things to events that have happened recently for our family or even that day for my child.

Wit and Humor

I mostly use dry humor (i.e. delivered without much overt emotion) in improv games. I try to avoid puns and minor humor that has a weak effect. Instead, I think a valuable type of wit emerges when you use material from the larger context of the game and interests of the child. One of the best ways of doing this is to try to resurface in new ways the things that were funny from earlier. But be cautious to not overuse that. In between those moments, I have found you can add humor by:

- Being absurdly random
- Being absurdly specific
- Being absurdly scientific

If your style of humor is more theatrical, you can use hyperbole with strong emotion to also get a comical effect. Just make sure you are not the only one laughing.

CHAPTER 11

Designing the Play Experience

Let's review what has been covered so far. In impromptu gameplay with your child:

- The child's role is to explore play courageously, which requires trusting you in your role.
- Your role is to love your child playfully, acting as a servant leader, like the Happy Host.
- It is your responsibility to keep your child engaged, avoiding disengagements like disparities, boredom, exhaustion, and discouragement.
- Your best tools for maintaining the fun are the artful use of anticipation, enlivening, and momentum, as well as the more calculated use of tensity and uncertainty.
- When it comes to amusements, the child can expect that something remarkable will happen, and the goal is to delight her.
- Games commonly follow a three-part game arc structure and involve competition between multiple players, rules that balance tensity, and the combination of skill, strategy, and chance.

This chapter looks at the broader picture of the whole playtime session, as well as special considerations for more deeply connecting with your child. It will help you to not only bring together the many concepts in this book, but also to play along with the child in the moment, all for the purpose of maximizing gameplay fun over the time available.

The Playtime Arc

A good way to visualize a playtime session is to consider playtime having its own arc with a beginning, a middle, and an end—much like the tilted bell curve of individual games and stories.

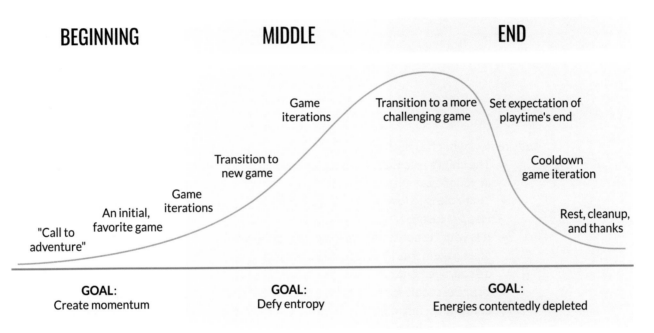

- The beginning has your call to adventure, where you invite the child into the initial game. The goal here is to create momentum.
- The middle includes transitions between iterations of a game and entirely new games. The goal here is to defy entropy while building momentum.
- The end is where you finally submit to entropy, with a goal of tapering out to a completion point where energies are contentedly depleted. In other words, the desire to continue roughly matches the desire to rest.

Why does this matter? This helps you suitably adjust things according to how much time is available, similar to how you might plan differently if you were running a sprint versus a marathon.

- If you have only a brief time to play, then choose high-intensity games that quickly generate momentum. Skip as many of the beginning elements as you can.
- If you can play for a long time, choose a collection of games that ease in and build up to high-intensity. This results in a better overall play experience (as opposed to peaking too early).

You don't have to plan everything out ahead of time—it is more about foreseeing the next, great game and being aware of roughly how much time remains.

Transitions

Seamlessly progressing from one game to the next is a major factor of momentum, one of the key ingredients of fun gameplay introduced in Chapter 7. Transitioning well requires intuition on when to transition and to what. Knowing which games to transition to requires testing out different sequences of games to see which combinations actually build momentum. Knowing when to transition requires keeping a keen awareness of the overall gameplay.

Timing Transitions

Aside from obvious transition points like completing a game or level, timing a good transition requires being tuned into the continuous feedback loop. The driver here is the manipulation of interest, so it is best if you can anticipate a transition near an interest peak. Otherwise, by the time you can clearly see a turning point in the child's interest, energy, or mood, you have already missed the ideal timing to act on it. However, that point is still not too late; it is too late when you have driven the child into the disengagements of boredom, exhaustion, or discouragement.

When you do decide to transition, do so efficiently to minimize the time between games (e.g. dead air). For example, if the next game will require some setup (e.g.

need to get the basket of blocks), try to stealthily begin the setup before the previous game is over, or fill in that setup time with a longer anticipation.

One exception to this is the **caesura effect**, where you deliberately, briefly, and subtly pause or suspend the flow of play to enable rest or heightened anticipation. A longer version of this can be done by choosing a game that reduces the tempo, such as when you mix in a mental challenge game after playing a series of strenuous games. At its longest, a caesura effectively resets the playtime arc and gives the child not only time to catch her breath but time to naturally prepare for the next game.

It is also important to know (and anticipate) when to end gameplay. I generally err on the side of going too long, because if we have had a great time playing together, it is not a big deal if it diminishes at the end. Ending too early or abruptly is much more frustrating for the child, perhaps even resulting in a tantrum. If you need to end early, you need to at least set expectations about there being "one more time," and preferably transition to a lower energy game to reduce momentum (and hence cause the game arc to descend).

Choosing the Next Step

Here are some common patterns for choosing what to transition to next. I often pick a game that allows me to be in the same or similar physical position without needing to change props. For example, Chestboard and Flipper go well together because you do not have to move anywhere, resulting in a quick transition. I have found that games in one position naturally transition well to games in other positions in the following ways:

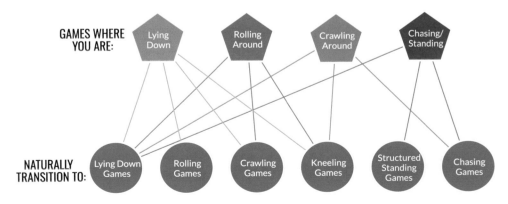

Natural Transitions

Lying-down games transition to:
- Other lying down games
- Rolling games
- Crawling games
- Kneeling games

Rolling games transition to:
- Lying down games
- Crawling games
- Kneeling games

Crawling games transition to:
- Lying down games
- Kneeling games
- Chasing games

Chasing games transition to:
- Structured standing games
- Lying down games
- Other chasing games

Here are some specific examples of position transitions, as well as other transitions that work because of certain atttributes they share.

Same Position Transitions
- Chestboard · Flipper
- Earthquake · Horsey
- Boom the Castle · Shoops
- The Weevil-Rat-Worm · The Poke of Death

Similar Position Transitions
- Bodybot · Rodeo
- Crib Wars · Battle Ball
- Narco Polo · Blind Monster Wrestline

Same Location Transitions
- Space Trash · Sitdown Game
- Most trampoline games

Similar Premise Transitions
- SpiderWalker · Horsey
- Levitate · Parkour
- Poke Music · The Poke of Death
- Traffic Circle · Centrifuge
- Krazy Fu · DodgeArm

Similar Prop Transitions
- Juggernaut · Lifeboat
- Balloon Soccer · Ninjaballoon
- Shinobi · Shoops

Natural Compliments
- Ticklebugs · chasing games
- Super Runs · Let's Jet
- Asteroids · Crusher (Crushim)

Tailored Gameplay

My kids are all at different ages and abilities, and so when we play together, I am always adapting the gameplay to each individual.

Age-Appropriate Play

Playing with infants is the pursuit of their delight; thus, delight activities are predominant, with all other game types coming later.

As they grow, toddlers will look for and enjoy following your lead in play, but I usually weave in their requests and game ideas, sticking to the principle of co-creation. Rapid repeatability and fast transitions are the norm for us, typically involving carpet tumbling, acrobatics, and child-climbing-all-over-me activities. Physical challenges are by far the most common type of games in this stage, and we are frequently experimenting with new games.

The imaginations of preschoolers and school-age children develop rapidly, not only enabling story to be woven into the enlivening, but enabling the enlivening to be a shared collaboration.

As they become older, they will want to jump right into their favorite games, being less interested in the tradition of the anticipation as they are interested in overcoming the physical, mental, or battle-based challenges in front of them.

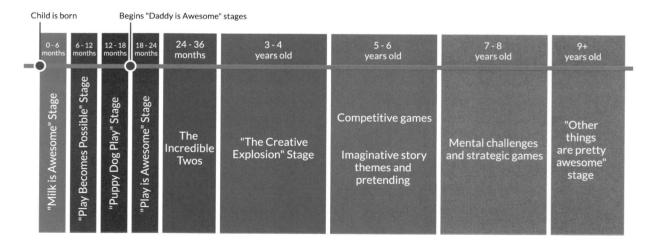

Here are the ages and stages of childhood play I have seen. This is based on my experience with my kids; your mileage might vary.

- **0** – child is born
- **0-6 months** – Milk is awesome stage, you have to work to make it laugh and even know that you exist
- **6-12 months** – "Play becomes possible" stage, the baby can't really do much yet, but a lightbulb goes off and it understands play. Lots of laughter starts. Peek-a-boo is a hit.
- **12-18 months** - "Puppy Dog Play" stage, where she wants to be chased, and roll around, and tumble. Lots of good touch, without the need for stunts or acrobatics. If you say "Ready, Set...", she will smile wide and brace herself. Immediately signs/says "more" after each turn.
- **18-24 months** – "Play is awesome" stage. Many more exciting/daring (while still simple) games become possible. She'll say, "ready, set, go" (right after saying/signing, "More")
  - This also marks the beginning of the "Daddy is Awesome" stage; they are always ready to play.
- **24-36 months** – The Incredible Twos, they come to you eager to play, lots of silly chasing, tickling, and acrobatic games get created.
- **3-4 yrs old** – The creative explosion. Perhaps the most playful time of all. Any object can turn into a plaything, any idea can become a game. More interesting game structures are now possible, allowing for a myriad of variations to good games.
- **5-6 yrs old** – More competitive and strategic games are now possible, including battles, accuracy-based and sport-based games, and more intricate building/destruction activities. Imaginative story themes and pretending blossom here.
- **7-8 yrs** – Mental challenges and game strategies become more interesting. You mainly return to the best classic games you've played together, rather than creating lots of new ones.
- **~9+ yrs** – "Other things are pretty awesome" stage. They won't turn down the opportunity to play with you, but the pull of friends, sports, and screens is mighty strong. As I write this, this is how old my oldest kids are, so I cannot speak knowledgeable beyond this.

Adaptations for Children with Special Needs

If you are a parent of a child with special needs, you already know better than I do how to accommodate her in play. Having a daughter with special needs has made me more aware of ways to make sure disabilities do not prevent anyone from sharing in the merrymaking.

What special needs?

The Happy Host is always adapting and adjusting play to the individual child—regardless of special needs. In other words, the adaptation principles are identical, such as the continuous feedback loop, tensity optimizations, and building momentum by avoiding boredom, exhaustion, and discouragement.

Compassionate Patience

It seems ingrained in us to want others to move at our pace, and we naturally become impatient when there is a pace disparity. A common example I see is when my daughter is "holding up the line" by taking her turn. While she is working her way steadily across the monkey bars, focusing on getting her mind and muscles to work together in a way that is second nature for her peers, I am managing the line of other kids, who are growing impatient. They invariably ask why it takes her so long. I simply say that she has to work harder at crossing the monkey bars than you do. She is not wasting anyone's time; she is capable of having fun and is pursuing it bravely, and we can accommodate for that.

Playing with children already requires a great deal of patience ("Okay, we can play that same game again and again…"), which most of us are willing to extend because we love our kids. But I believe the type of patience I have for my daughter with special needs stems from a more compassionate understanding of the individual—a patience born out of appreciation, not pity.

Lovingkindness

And at other times it is just a patience born out of fatherly love. At bedtime each night, my daughter enjoys pulling the sheets over her head and pretending she has disappeared. She does this almost every night, and every night my response is of course to pretend to panic and look for her, eventually finding her as she giggles, kissing her, and continuing our bedtime routine. I make it a point to always give a unique response. ["Oh man, now I need to go get a new Whitney and there is no way it will be as good as the original." "Wow, this bed is bumpy. I better smash down these bumps before Whitney comes back." "Oh no. I better sit down and file a missing child report with the authorities." "I knew I shouldn't have left my cross-dimensional shrink ray gun unattended."] That is how I keep a comfortably familiar pleasure fresh and enjoyable for her (and interesting to us both), even when the whole thing feels repetitious and timeworn to me. She's worth it.

Open Arms

Another pattern I see is in how some children use me as a translator for her by asking me a question about her instead of turning to her and asking her directly. ["Does she like tag?" "That's a good question. Go ahead and ask her."] And unfortunately I often see some children exhibit Game Bully tendencies around her. For example, kids will often make her be the monster (the whole time) or not let her join in at all. These are good kids, but they are just uncomfortable with what is unfamiliar. You need to step in here as the Happy Host, welcome her in, and demonstrate to others that she is a full person.

Adaptations for Groups

I love to play with just one child at a time, but fun is like a magnet that pulls in additional kids as they become aware that Daddy is playing right now. Here are some tips on how to accommodate multiple kids as group play forms.

- Safety is a real concern
  - Each game has a sensible limit in how many kids can actively participate.
  - Kids can be reckless and crash into each other. Warnings and rules are of some value, but you need to be on the ready to step in and avert big mishaps.
- Set up teams or a line for turn-taking
  - The best way to reduce the chaos is to either divide up the group into teams or reduce how many individuals are active at once. See

the player arrangments patterns in Chapter 9 for some ideas.

- This comes at the expense of each kid's active playtime, so keep turns fairly short so bystanders remain engaged.
- Also make sure bystanders are physically out of the way of the main action.
- Do not ease up on your responsibilities unless you intentionally want the kids to play together without you.

What Really Matters

As wonderful as fun and laughter are, ultimately your kids just want to be with you, experience that they matter to you, and know that you love them no matter what. That is a phrase I continually ingrain in them.

> *I love you no matter what.*
> *That means there's nothing you can do to make me love you less; you can't lose my love. It also means there's nothing you can do to make me love you more; you can't earn my love.*

Play is a wonderful occasion to express all of this, supplementing our words with laughter and touch. This can all be summed up in how it started, in how I see my noble purpose as a father, and how I challenge you to be fun: love your kids playfully. In doing so you will find your own authentic style and create a lot of treasured memories.

As for us, after years of hijinks, I find pleasure in seeing my kids start to use these techniques as they play with each other and other children. And someday, God willing, when I am an old man and we are looking back fondly, I hope we say, "Let's do that again." And we will—or at least we will look through this book again because I'll be an old man and playing Chestboard at that stage would probably be fatal.

APPENDIX

The Hall of Forgotten Games

This is a list of games from long ago for which I only wrote down the name and now can only guess at what they were. Perhaps they will spur you on to fun new games.

- I Only Hear the Blanket
- Don't Cross the Line
- Flying Pancake
- Kiss Duel
- Throw Jonah from the Boat
- Storm Running
- Don't Shake the Baby
- Flap-hands Knockdown
- Poisonous Frog Pretend
- Corkscrew of Death
- Pillow Knockdown
- Kissing Dragon (trampoline)
- Balloon Robot Slicer
- Mind the Gap (mattress)
- Slow Approaching Giant
- Animal Transform by Touch
- That's Mine!
- Don't Drop Me
- Gauntlet
- Battle Billiards
- Flying Reindeer
- Piranha
- Bruiser
- Waylayer
- Wiggles
- Pitfall Mattress
- Navigator
- Dogpile
- Magic Rabbit
- Carbonite
- Slow Punch
- Toro
- Jumpleg
- Catcher
- Bounce Balloon
- Pushover
- Roll the Can
- Smush on Couch
- Lava Rocks
- Foot Wrestle
- Rocker Hopper
- Throw the Balloon at the Giant
- Foot Launcher
- Run and Jump Line
- Gladiator Football
- Prize Grabber
- Rocket Tower
- Mattress Bounce
- Jetway (with mattress pump)
- Blowout
- Tube Ninja
- Trip the Giant
- Toes on the Carpet
- Running of the Dylan
- Throw Lava Ball
- Tunnels
- Unleashed
- Pirate Asteroids
- Send You to the Moon

Glossary

Amusements: Simple, non-competitive, gameplay activities involving basic cause and effect actions or acrobatics, where something remarkable happens, such as a moment's delight.

Anticipation: Initiating the gameplay well for optimal fun. It is the initial stage of games and amusements that communicates something remarkable is about to happen.

Battles: Competitive games and contests with the goal of overcoming the opponent. These are generally head-to-head duels, without turn taking, where there is a struggle for victory, though generally not a prize.

Boredom: Mental fatigue in hoping for an improvement that just does not come, leaving the child disappointed with what is already in hand.

Broken play: Gameplay that has been intentionally interrupted by actions of poor character, such as rudely stealing the ball from the youngest player out of jealousy.

Cattle prodding: Aggressive tickling that might be momentarily stimulating but quickly thereafter unpleasant (and depending on the child unwelcome).

Cause-pause: The pause between the cause and the effect of an amusement, which intensifies the tension by creating an emotional buildup that will be converted to delight.

Caesura effect: Deliberately, briefly, and subtly pausing or suspending the flow of play to enable rest or heightened anticipation.

Clarifying rules: Game rules introduced as needed after gameplay has already started as a way of evolving the gameplay into something better (as opposed to restarting broken gameplay).

CIMIOA: "Can I make it out alive?" The critical moment of self-doubt at the end of a game's complication when the child is not sure she will achieve the desired outcome after all.

Complication: The middle section of a game when a rising challenge emerges. The result of the complication is a moment of deep self-doubt (the CIMIOA).

Continuous feedback loop: To carefully listen and then respond in creative kindness. Using situational awareness to help you determine if the gameplay needs something more, or less, or something different, then incorporating the principles of gameplay, your intimate knowledge of the child, and your own creative contributions before deciding how you will respond.

Daunting taunting: A voice portrayal when enlivening that is used to create a sense of urgency by taking up the voice of the villain, making it more exciting for the child to imagine from whom or what she is running. ("Get her! Don't let her escape!", "You'll never get away with this!")

Delight: A brief emotional elation, which usually makes us laugh or even happily scream out of sudden excitement.

Delight spirals: Iterating on an amusement, rather than just repeating it, seeking to reach a higher level of delight in each loop.

Delights: A category of gameplay that consists of simple amusements with the focus of giving the child temporary elation.

Discouragement: Being emotionally convinced you are doomed to fail, losing hope of meaningful participation and fun. When discouraged, a child resigns from gameplay or acts out in frustration.

Disparities: A type of gameplay entropy that occurs when there is a disappointing mismatch in expectations between you and your child. From the child's perspective, it is a quick letdown from what he thought would happen to what actually occurred.

Enlivening: Using theatrics and sound effects to bring the game to life.

Entering sudden reality: Enlivening a game by immediately portraying a character in character.

Entropy: The reality that gameplay, by itself, will always eventually diminish. The four types of gameplay entropy are disparities, boredom, exhaustion, and discouragement.

Essential rules: Game rules that if you did not state up front, you would have to interrupt the gameplay to explain.

Exhaustion: Physical fatigue from continuous exertion in gameplay.

Expectation: The initial stage of a game when you establish the setting, the objective, and the rules. It should result in each player having an exciting plan for what is about to happen and an inflated confidence.

Fulfillment: The concluding stage of a game that resolves the built-up physical and emotional tension through a central amusement, followed by the outcome and a transition hook.

Fun: A sense of enjoyment, one step above satisfaction, resulting from a reflection on an experience that was entertaining and fulfilling, such as when the result of a game is even better than what you expected.

Game arc: The general lifecycle of a game, having a beginning (the expectation), a middle (the complication), and an end (the fulfillment).

Game Bully: A gameplay role to avoid, characterized by demanding your own way with disregard for the kid's level of enjoyment.

Game Chaperone: A gameplay role to avoid, characterized by watching from a distance, being primarily concerned that no one gets hurt and that gametime ends on time.

Game Clown: A gameplay role to avoid, characterized by "performing for" rather than "playing with" kids; entertaining everyone with constant over-the-top theatrics and silliness.

Game Conqueror: A gameplay role to avoid, characterized by being overly competitive and sometimes physically reckless in pursuit of your own fun and glory.

Game Lawyer: A gameplay role to avoid, characterized by enumerating too many rules in pursuit of supreme fairness, or trying to be the ultimate referee and legislator.

Game Wimp: A gameplay role to avoid, characterized by being passive, uninspired, and unprepared in gameplay, avoiding decisions and responding without opinion.

Games: Structured activities, ranging from simple to complex, that are generally competitive and involve skill, strategy, and chance.

Happy Host: A servant leadership role in gameplay where you take charge without taking over.

Line of uncertainty: The boundary between an amusement's cause and effect, marking the end of the cause-pause.

Manipulation of interest: Nimble management of the child's interest, such as by shifting her focus or dynamically increasing tensity, to keep the child continuously engaged and to build momentum.

Mental challenges: Games where the most interesting challenge is more mental than physical.

Momentum: Transitioning well within and between games, generally building up a great playtime experience.

Oblivious observer: A voice portrayal when enlivening characterized by enacting an almost blind character that cannot see precisely the thing he is looking for (which is usually the child). ("This chair seems lumpy...")

Physical challenges: Games where the focus is on using skill or strength to accomplish a goal.

Play: Mutually amusing my young kids with impromptu, usually one-on-one games and amusements.

Playtime arc: The general lifecycle of an entire play session, visualized as having a beginning, a middle, and an end.

Portrayal: Acting, representing something dramatically by using your voice, body movements, and timing.

Pre-game anticipations are used to announce the transition into a game, and they generally are used only once because they are either too monotonous or non-sequitur to use after the game has begun.

Pre-play anticipations initiate (or conclude) the play iteration, usually taking the form of a recognizable phrase that is specific to that game. They are common in rapidly repeatable games like Ooga Booga and Cage that Animal.

Rapid repeatability: Iterating on the main amusement pattern with little to no restart time, such as when you send additional asteroids and when you restart Ooga Booga by using its hook phrase.

Squire crier: A voice portrayal when enlivening used to assist the child by providing vital hints or unseen context. ("Look out!", "Quick, grab the sword!")

Situational awareness: Whatever feedback you can gather in the moment regarding the game, the players, and the environment.

Superpowers: Activities where you augment the child's capabilities in a fantastic way, such as by removing limitations or amplifying current capabilities.

Tensity: Balancing the right level of difficulty so that the outcome of the challenge is perceived to be achievable yet uncertain.

Tiered tensity: Iteratively increasing a game's tensity so that each iteration is only slightly more complex or difficult than the previous one.

Transitions: Progressing from one game or game iteration to the next. Seamless transitions are a major factor of momentum.

Tyrant: A child who oppressively controls the direction and rules of the game, like a child version of the Game Bully.

Uncertainty: Keeping things from being too predictable.

Vicarious exclamations: A voice portrayal when enlivening that is used to intensify the action by vocalizing the thoughts you would imagine saying if you were in the child's situation. ("Oh no! Oh the agony! It's eating my flesh!")

My daughter's self portrait on her first day of preschool.

Learn more and share your games and stories at:

HTTPS://LDTA.REDEVISED.COM

Seize the
Play!

Made in the USA
Columbia, SC
28 May 2025

58574049R00115